THE MY~ ~

Dear Kevin

I remember so
much from the past
that is best forgotten
and so much that I
still treasure. The gratuities
fall into both categories

Hugh.

THE
MYTHS OF TIME

From Saint Augustine to *American Beauty*

HUGH RAYMENT-PICKARD

Qoheleth tried to write in an attractive style
and set down truthful thoughts in a straight-
forward manner.

(Ecclesiastes 12:10, *Jerusalem Bible*)

DARTON·LONGMAN + TODD

for Don Cupitt

First published in 2004 by
Darton, Longman and Todd Ltd
1 Spencer Court
140–142 Wandsworth High Street
London SW18 4JJ

© 2004 Hugh Rayment-Pickard

ISBN 0 232 52493 9

A catalogue record for this book is available
from the British Library.

Designed by Sandie Boccacci
Phototypeset in 9.25/12.75pt Stone Serif by Intype Libra Ltd
Printed and bound in Great Britain by
The Cromwell Press, Trowbridge, Wiltshire

CONTENTS

PREFACE AND ACKNOWLEDGEMENTS

This book emerges from fifteen years of writing, teaching and thinking about philosophical theology and the philosophy of history. Over this time, I came to agree strongly with those who believe that an understanding of time and history is basic to all theology and philosophy. We are always living time. Indeed we are time. So the question of time's meaning needs to be central to any investigation or theory of what it is to be human.

Time did not seem to me to be a 'philosophical' or 'theological' issue in the narrow sense of these terms. The question of time is a *human* issue that doesn't belong in any one academic category. So I have sought to draw eclectically upon ideas, arguments and images from a broad range of sources: film, fiction, philosophy, theology, psychoanalysis, sociology, poetry and illustrations from everyday life. I have tried to write this book as an essay in the *ars vivendi* or the art of living. Theology and philosophy should be tools for human living. This book tries to *use* philosophy and theology, as Nietzsche put it, 'in the service of life', to bring these and other disciplines to bear upon a crucial human question: what do we mean by 'time'?

I decided fairly early on not to deal with the science of time. This has already been very well summarised by people properly qualified to do it – such as Paul Davis in his excellent *About Time* (Penguin, 1995). In any case, this book concerns the human *meaning* of time, an issue that falls outside scientific investigation.

I was immensely lucky at various stages in planning and writing to be able to seek the advice and suggestions of others, particularly Linda Woodhead, Giles Fraser and Phillip Lankester. Don Cupitt, Rachel Carr and Alan Everett offered me invaluable critical comments on the whole book. I am grateful to all of them for their friendship, which I prize very greatly. My wife Liz was my most honest but most loving critic and I am deeply grateful for all her support and indeed for the encouragement and patience of Henry and Alexandra my children and of my whole family.

I owe an incalculable debt of gratitude to Don Cupitt, to whom this book is dedicated. For twenty years I have been inspired, encouraged and provoked by his writings and through his friendship.

I am grateful to the Diocese of London, Sion College, Emmanuel College Cambridge and the Parish of St Clement and St James for grants which enabled me to take time away from parish work to research this book.

All biblical quotations are from the Revised Standard Version unless otherwise indicated.

HUGH RAYMENT-PICKARD

PROLOGUE

Our inner duration, considered from the first to the
last moment of our conscious life, is something like . . .
melody.

(Henri Bergson, *Duration and Simultaneity*)

The real presence of Time in the World is called *Man*.
Time *is* Man, and Man *is* Time.

(Alexandre Kojève, *Introduction to the Reading of Hegel*)

What are days for?

'What are days for?' asks Philip Larkin in his poem 'Days'. His
answer is as simple as it is profound: 'Days are where we live.' For
some reason we tend to think of our lives in terms of space, of
being in places and moving *between* places. But space is only half
of it, we also live in time. We are located in days and between
days: we are always datable. Today, as I write this very sentence I
am located at 6.46pm on 5 December 2002. You reading this same
sentence are located elsewhere in time. I am communicating with
you over a distance that is as real as the gap between London and
New York, but we cannot see the gap. The 'gaps' between locations
in time are very strange. They are invisible, non-spatial, more like
thoughts than things.

We do know that the gaps are asymmetrical, open only at one
end. From your end, you can look back to me, or hear me, across
the gap. But the gap is screened-off on my side. From my location,
you are in the future. I cannot see you, whoever you are, wherever you are, whatever date you are. And there may be many of
you, distributed across time. And your time location keeps moving,
even when you are standing still. The distance between us keeps
stretching, always longer, never shorter, so that even as you read

these words, you are disappearing into the time-distance, like a ball drifting out to sea. You have been drifting your whole life. Wherever you are located, wherever you are drifting in time, this book is our connection, what we have between us. What you are reading is a trace from my time location, a message from December 2002, a message in time, about time.

Just over a century ago, the French philosopher Henri Bergson developed a concept designed to help us to understand our relationship with time: Bergson called time 'lived duration'. The mistake we make when we think about time is to imagine that time is just an environment within which our thoughts and experience take place. So we think of time as happening outside us, as though we were standing in the middle of a busy road with time speeding past.

But we are not *inside* time, we *are* time, our very thoughts and actions are not only an experience *of* time but the very happening of time itself. This time, the on-going lived duration of our experience is what Bergson called 'real time'. Bergson gave this illustration: Imagine moving your finger across the surface of a piece of paper. If you watch your finger move it would appear that this line represents the time your finger took to move across the page. Since this line is measurable and divisible into units, it would seem that time itself can be measured and divided. But this external, visible picture of time is an illusion. Time is not happening on the outside, argued Bergson, but on the inside of experience. So imagine again drawing the same line, but this time with your eyes closed. Try to feel the full experience – the texture of the paper fibres against your finger, the action of your arm, the temperature of the air and the noises around. This total experience of sensations, thoughts and feelings is the 'unfolding' of lived duration which is not a simple line but a complex layering of simultaneous processes that cannot be divided into measurable sections. This 'duration', where time 'unfolds' like polyphonic music (one of Bergson's favourite analogies), is where we live and move and have our being. 'Duration' is what we really are.

Days are where we live, we drifters in time. But what do we do with our days? What attitude do we have towards the 27,500 days that make up the duration of an average human life? What does the time of our lives mean? What are these few thousands of days for? Where are we drifting? What is the purpose and shape of our ever-dwindling allocation of time?

There are many possible answers to these questions and this book is an exploration of the ways in which we have imagined the shape and meaning of time, our time, the duration of our lives. These shapes form something like a 'grammar' of time. This grammar not only enables us to think about the structure of time but it helps us to understand its *inflection*. By 'inflection' I mean that time has moods: hope and despair, fullness and emptiness, boredom and excitement, waiting and completion. The following chapters will attempt to explore how time has been shaped and inflected both within our religious traditions and beyond them.

The time of your life

> The optimist builds himself safe inside a cell
> And paints the inside walls sky blue
> And blocks up the door
> And says he's in heaven.
>
> (D. H. Lawrence, 'The Optimist')

> I have been studying how I may compare
> This prison where I live unto the world.
>
> (Shakespeare, *Richard II*)

> In the cell . . . you are the master of time and of your thinking.
>
> (Jean Genet, *Miracle of the Rose*)

In order to begin thinking about the shape and inflection of time, consider this imaginary situation: You are on your summer holidays and have the misfortune to be captured by mysterious kidnappers. You are locked in a bare room and told that you will have to remain there for 'as long as it takes'. You are not told what your captors want, but you are told that you will not be released unless their demands are met. One thing they do say (and they don't say much) is that they are prepared to detain you for the rest of your life. Although the room is generally featureless, there is a roof-light with bars through which you can see a small patch of sky.

You now face an indefinite period before your release or your death – whichever comes sooner. You must now fill your time (however long that is) with *something*. You must now decide what your attitude is to your time and what you propose to do. It's not for nothing that prisoners speak of 'doing time'. Time is now your task.

At the back of your mind is a terrible thought: perhaps your captors are just sadists who have locked you up for fun. Perhaps there are no 'demands' and no way out. Perhaps these twisted bastards just want to watch you rot. Perhaps your situation is *already* catastrophic. In which case there is no hope of release. Perhaps they will tell you this one day, just to see how you take it. Your time is now meaningless. 'Your' time is really their time: you just have to endure it. You think of suicide – that would be one small piece of control. Or perhaps you could find meaning by colluding with your captors – join their game and play the role of doomed prisoner. In this 'catastrophic' frame of mind you look up at the patch of sky and see it as a taunt, a cruel reminder that there is No Way Out. Time feels like decay – you can sense your life wasting away. Whatever you do, it seems your time is headed for oblivion. At night you pray, cursing God for your predicament.

Not all your days in the cell are as bad as this. Your attitude becomes more positive when you try to plan your escape. You weigh up the options. You could dig a tunnel or try to force the bars on the roof-light. Perhaps you could overcome the guards or trick them. Maybe you could persuade them to release you, using clever arguments. You decide on the tunnel, loosening a stone from the wall so that you can scrape through the earth behind it with the spoon you have stolen from the meal tray. Each night you replace the stone and each day the tunnel lengthens. It's currently three metres long! Planning your escape feels good. Time feels *productive*. There's a point to everything you do, and every minute seems to be heading somewhere. You are sustained by a vision of your freedom and the patch of sky symbolises the light at the end of the tunnel. At night you pray for the strength to dig harder in the morning.

It may be hard to keep up your motivation and morale. When

will the tunnel reach its end? 5 metres? 10 metres? 100 metres? Will there ever be an end? It's clear to you that tunnelling also involves waiting and hope. The work on the tunnel makes you impatient, and you have to teach yourself how to wait. How to sit in the dark hours and not panic. The time of waiting is hard. The working hours fly by and seem to have a point. But an hour waiting can feel like empty time: blank minutes following blank minutes. Waiting requires mental discipline, because you must remain vigilant in expectation of an end. Above all you need faith: faith that the tunnel will lead to freedom. 'Waiting time' is on permanent stand-by, all dressed up with nowhere to go, it's time on sentry duty, or stuck in a queue. In moments of waiting, the patch of sky represents your distant hope. And at night you pray for the end to come quickly: maranatha, maranatha.

One morning a shaft of sunlight shoots through the roof-light. The bars cause the shadow of a cross to be cast on the wall and around it the plaster is bathed in light. The plaster looks beautiful: pink like coral and luminous like the face of a child. The moment seems to be timeless, an epiphany of meaning that compensates for every aching hour working in the tunnel and every desolate minute waiting in the night. You ask the guards for a pen and paper and start to write a poem. You want to keep this moment, bottle it, so that you can savour it again. After this, you resolve to seek out everything that is good about your present situation: the fresh smell of the soil in the tunnel; the antics of insects on the walls and floor; the simple stillness of the night hours. You try to build a relationship with the guards. You decorate the walls with pictures, ideas, crazy doodles. And sometimes you think up ironic prisoner jokes, laughing out loud to the bafflement of your captors. These moments of beauty and joy seem to transfigure time. Time now feels like a series of opportunities for wonder, laughter and relationships. Why bother with the tunnel? Life is here and now. Why hope for greater freedom in the future when there are so many freedoms to be found in this very room? You let time acquiesce in the present, in stillness, giving in to what is already there, what is already possible. You let the beatitude of 'now' be your comfort. The patch of sky represents the sanctity and beauty of every moment. You stare at it, not with longing, not in hope, but in meditation. And at night you pray to God with thanksgiving, counting your blessings.

One day you are in the process of writing a sonnet about the flaking plaster on the wall, when your captors open the door with the message that their demands have been met and you are to be released. They apologise for any inconvenience caused and drop you back at your holiday hotel. That evening you reflect upon your captivity and your changing attitudes to time. When you were in despair time seemed to be eating you away, without hope, without purpose. Your feelings of despair were real and it was always *possible* that your situation really was hopeless. It would be all but impossible to stay in this mood and remain sane. So to escape despair you had to believe, somehow, that your time in the room had meaning. Looking back you see that there were three ways in which you had made time meaningful: First, you made time *purposeful*, by working on the tunnel. Secondly, you made time *hopeful* by learning how to wait in expectation. Thirdly, you made time *beautiful* by finding happiness in the present moment. Perhaps the ideal attitude to time would be a combination of all three: to find purpose, hope *and* beauty in time. You make a mental note to try combining your time attitudes, ready for the next situation when the structure and meaning of your time is in question. No sooner have you made this note than you wonder whether that 'next situation' is now.

The point of this 'thought experiment' is to strip away many of the particular details of life in order to focus precisely on how we think about time. Real life is not a prison, but we do live within a given space, with given resources and a given time. We do need to decide, deliberately or by default, what attitude to take to time. If we reflect upon time, we realise that people respond in distinctive ways. Some tend to despair of life and can make no sense of it. Others tend to see time as productive and busy themselves in projects and schemes. Some believe you have to wait for good things to happen rather than working for them. And others seek satisfaction and meaning from the ongoing present moment. All of us will tend, temperamentally and at different times, towards one mode or another. This book is an attempt to classify and discuss the various ways in which we have pictured time and to show how the different models of time are found both in Christianity and in secular art and literature.

I am calling the first model of time – which is basic to all the others – the Catastrophic or C type mode of time. C type time is a process of dissipation or ruin that ends badly and without meaning. The second mode of time is sceptical about human endeavours and prefers to remain open to the arrival of meaning rather than trying to force meaning upon history. I call this Apocalyptic or A type time because it waits for 'revelation' (the literal meaning of 'apocalypse'). The third model seeks to find meaning in time as it happens, to transfigure time momentarily in art, liturgy or through acts of love. I have called this Kairic or K type time after the Greek word *kairos*, a term used by Jesus to mean time as 'opportunity'. Finally, the fourth mode seeks to redeem time through work. I call this Prophetic or P type time because it projects forward (prophesies) a desired end to history and then works towards it.

The purpose of this scheme of four types of time is to provide a path through an extremely slippery subject. But no scheme can ever do justice to the ambiguities and complexities of the 'lived duration' of human existence. Any reductive model should be treated like Wittgenstein's ladder: once you've climbed it, you should push it away.

CHAPTER ONE

Introduction: Beyond Coherence

The world's biggest jigsaw

In the middest, we look for a fullness of time,
for beginning, middle and end in concord.
(Frank Kermode, The Sense of an Ending)

Reality . . . is a perpetual becoming. It makes or remakes
itself, but it is never something made.
(Henri Bergson, The Creative Mind)

Each life is an encylopaedia, a library,
an inventory of objects, a series of styles.
(Italo Calvino, Six Memos for the Next Millennium)

Dissonance
(if you're interested)
leads to discovery.
(William Carlos Williams, Paterson IV)

Christianity has traditionally thought that all the pieces of our experience must 'fit together' like the world's biggest jigsaw. From our point of view life looks like a jumble of bits and pieces, some coherent, some contradictory, some frankly incomprehensible. But that – we are told – is just because we are not very good at metaphysical jigsaws. We see the pieces, not the full picture. If only we could see things correctly, logically and coherently, we would see that everything in life is part of one picture, one truth, and one reality.

Christian doctrine has been modelled on a belief in the Ultimate Coherence of everything in a single cosmic jigsaw. Missing bits, spare bits, misshapen bits are not allowed. Everything must fit perfectly without omissions or extras. A place for everything, everything in its place and everything under control. This, so we are told, is how God wants it to be. He doesn't like mess or ambiguity. God likes everything to fit together just so.

This is hard for us to understand. How, for example, do opposites like good and evil both find their place in one coherent picture? St Augustine came up with a clever but unconvincing explanation: the 'evil' bits of the jigsaw are not real bits of jigsaw at all. If we could look at the puzzle as a whole, we would see that the picture is perfect and that the apparently ill-fitting pieces are just the empty spaces at the edge where the picture finishes. 'Taken singly, each thing is good; but collectively they are very good' (*Confessions*, XIII, 32). Over the centuries Christian theologians have devised many other ingenious defences of the Ultimate Coherence of everything. Some say we just need faith in coherence. Others say that there is a struggle underway to bring about Ultimate Coherence. Others say that cosmic coherence is like music that can make even dissonant notes sound part of the harmony.

A more radical solution to the problem is to abandon the jigsaw paradigm. Perhaps it is not helpful to think in terms of Ultimate Coherence. Perhaps the true picture of the world includes anomalies, contradictions, gaps and discontinuities. Perhaps the world appears in many and various true pictures. Perhaps 'non-coherence' is the truth of things. If this is so, we need not one but a range of theoretical perspectives and a repertoire of theologies. If the truth really is complex, then an excessive concern with coherence would be an unhelpful attitude.

This is not to say that there is no such thing as truth, but it does require us to think of 'truth' differently. There is perhaps a *more true* view of truth than the view that all things must lock together into a single picture. The truth of plurality and excess is arguably a higher truth than the idea of Ultimate Coherence. Life is multifarious, fluid and contradictory and a theology of complexity is simply more faithful to our experience.

The belief in Ultimate Coherence is really just a prejudice in favour of orderliness. There is nothing inherently *right* about this prejudice. But when a prejudice is held long enough and passionately enough, it can appear like an unshakeable truth. One of the functions of philosophy is to disturb prejudice and show us other ways of thinking.

Let's forget the jigsaw and imagine that the world is inherently eclectic, like a wide-ranging art gallery. Here we have many pictures, not one. They hang together in a single space, but they are of different styles and emerge from different viewpoints. There is no point in trying to amalgamate them into one giant picture because they do not belong together in that way. To appreciate an art gallery properly we must understand and value *difference*. That's what's interesting and exciting: there is more than one valid 'take' on the world. This book is written in the belief that the world is more like an art gallery than a jigsaw, that the truth is indeed plural, and that a complex of theological and other perspectives is required to make sense of life.

The complex of time

> . . . May God us keep
> From single vision . . .
>
> (William Blake, 'With
Happiness stretch'd across the hills')

> The sand of the sea, the drops of rain,
> and the days of eternity –
> who can count them?
>
> (Ecclesiasticus 1:2, *NRSV*)

Very early in the process of researching this book I realised that the Christian view of time was not a single doctrine but a plait of contesting myths about human destiny. The teaching of Jesus about time does not reduce to an ultimately coherent view. At times Jesus implies that time is fulfilled in the present moment; at others he indicates that the fulfilment of time has yet to come. At times he says that we can work to help bring about the future; at others he says we must simply await the arrival of the kingdom. In the Old Testament there is a range of prophetic, apocalyptic and mystical views about time. And there is a radical, unbridgeable difference between the theology of time in Paul's letter to the Romans and that offered in the letter to the Ephesians. The French thinker Paul Ricoeur reaches a similar conclusion. Ricoeur argues that what we mean by 'biblical time' is an 'interweaving of temporalities of different qualities': narrative time, legislative time, prophetic time, the time of wisdom and hymnic time. 'Biblical time' is all these different things at once.

It would require a violation of the text – a *desecration* if you like – to hammer all these views into a coherent whole. In order to respect the biblical thinking of time, I would have to respect its multiplicity and non-coherence. The task I set myself was to try to show how multiple, contesting views of time can 'belong' together in a way that is more powerful – and more truthful – than a single, totalising doctrine. The task was not to show how the different views clicked together like jigsaw pieces, or to show how the differences could be reduced to a unified view. Rather, the task was to describe the biblical view of time in terms of internal tensions, differences, contradictions and interactions. I needed to find a way to elaborate what Jorge Louis Borges (in a different context) called 'the garden of forked paths': a 'growing and bewildering network of divergent, convergent and parallel forms of time'. One phrase that came to mind was Paul's reference to 'the fullness of time' – not a fullness of uniformity, but a fullness of multiplicity.

This approach is strange, but not entirely alien, to Christian theology. The doctrines of the Trinity and the two natures of Christ have traditionally allowed for some sense of inherent complexity. But this complexity has always been harmonious – like the voices in baroque counterpoint. What I wanted to describe was a less harmonious complexity – the combination not just of different melodies, but different genres of music – different in mood, style and tempo. Together they might form 'a collection' or 'a cluster', but not a harmonic whole. Considering them together one could speak meaningfully of 'similarity' and 'difference' but not of 'coherence'.

Another metaphor that came to mind was that of the plait: a rope made of many strands. These strands are twisted together but they are all separate. The strands may be of clashing colours, materials and thickness. Each strand may be unwound and used in its own right. Yet there is an additional strength in being bound together. The Christian view of time is something like this: an interlacing of independent threads. And, like a rope, what holds the threads together is *friction*.

It would be interesting to explore this theology of dissonance and non-coherence on a much broader scale, searching out the abrasions, tensions, fault lines and contradictions that play their part in structuring all aspects of Christian theology. This book, however, will have to restrict itself to the non-coherence within 'the Christian view of time'.

So '*the* Christian view of time' is really a complex of views, a matrix of possibilities. We cannot 'subscribe' to the Christian view of time as if it were a take-it-or-leave-it proposition that required support or refutation. To be within 'the Christian tradition' is to be part of a debate or conversation in which many contradictory voices are simultaneously necessary and correct. The person who says 'the present is everything, just live in the moment' is as correct as the person who says 'the future is everything, sacrifice every present moment to achieve it'. The conflict between these views can't be squared away – and it doesn't need to be. We simply need to accept the character of the Christian tradition as non-coherence. This tradition is an unbounded, fluid and multi-levelled cultural domain that can no longer prescribe religious life for us, but can only offer symbols, models, practices and possibilities. As such, the tradition cannot lay down the law for us. At best it can only set out some parameters for discussion, showing us options and alternatives. The tradition acts as a resource rather than a precept.

This book is an attempt to explore the resources of the long and varied traditions of Christian thinking on time. In order to uncover the differences and tensions between the separate strands of thinking about time I have drawn upon insights and ideas from the philosophy of history, in particular from so-called 'narrativist' philosophy of history. Instead of trying to describe history itself, the narrativists looked at the types of story we tell about the past, and the ways in which these stories are 'emplotted'. Following this approach – developed in various ways by such thinkers as Roland Barthes, Paul Ricoeur, Northrop Frye and Hayden White – I have used some narrativist methods in order to discuss time.

I will argue that we know very little about time and that the relevant human question is not what time is, but how it is narrated. So the strands of thinking about time are strands of narrative or types of story. However, these narrative strands are not 'theories' about time, but modes of being in time, actual living states of existence. Being in time is something we can feel physically with every breath. The narrative strands of time are living stories. We do not experience time as an idea, but as the visceral happening of life itself. Time is, as Bergson described it, lived duration. But this duration is sculpted and textured into different narrative shapes.

This book offers a schematic classification of four kinds of story about time: Stories of catastrophe, apocalypse, opportunity and prophecy. Each story has its own distinctive structure and mood. Each story creates its own *Zeitgestalt*, or time-shape. Within each *Zeitgestalt* time is understood and experienced in a distinctive way. There is, for example, 'a world of difference' – indeed 'a difference of world' – between a story structured around apocalyptic waiting and a story structured around historical progress. These are incompatible narrative forms. People living out these kinds of stories act in quite different ways and for different reasons. It is not possible to collapse these stories together to produce one structure, one sense of time, and one kind of human activity. Or rather, it is possible – but only as an act of violence. Unfortunately Christian theology has often been responsible for such forced reductions of difference and variety.

This four-fold scheme seemed to me to mark out the main differences in approach that we find in the Bible. But this classification is not dogmatic and I considered alternative schemes before fixing on this one. There are certainly sub-categories within these four genres (some of which I explore) and it could be argued that these constitute separate strands in their own right.

The biblical views of time, however, were not the point of arrival but the point of departure for this exploration. The ways of thinking of time in the Bible seemed to me to be echoed or repeated in our contemporary culture. The strands of thinking about time that make up the ancient Christian plait seemed to reappear in new configurations, with new emphases, in our secular and perhaps post-Christian age. So this book is also an attempt to account for the relevance of Christianity in recent Western culture, to show that allegedly 'modern' ways of thinking about time draw upon much earlier patterns of thought. I will argue, for example, that Samuel Beckett repeats (in a different way) the apocalyptic time-view of St Paul; and that our post-modern ideas of 'real time' repeat the ancient Greek understanding of 'opportunity'.

In this way, I would like to challenge the pervasive assumption that modernity must always go hand-in-hand with novelty. Is there another way of being 'modern' that does not require incessant innovation? Is it possible now – as it was in the Renaissance – to be modern partly through the reworking of the ideas of the past? Is there a more rooted way of being modern that seeks out continuity with earlier traditions? This would be modernity-with-a-backward glance, not modernity versus heritage, but modernity with heritage. The Renaissance poet Francis Petrarch tried to analyse areas of his life by writing an imaginary dialogue between himself and St Augustine. At other times he tussled with Seneca and Virgil. These dialogues seemed as natural to him as talking with his contemporaries. This book will make similar journeys back and forth between earlier traditions and our own thinking of time.

Narrative realism

There isn't a True account of time; the way you experience the time of your life depends upon the way you choose to live. A treatise about time recommends a way of life.

(Don Cupitt, *The Time Being*)

Time becomes human to the extent that it is organized after the manner of a narrative.

(Paul Ricoeur, *Time and Narrative*)

Rather than pass the time, we must invite it in.

(Walter Benjamin, *Arcades Project*)

So the meaning of time is generated within some basic narrative time forms. What we mean by 'time' depends how we narrate its passage. Our world of time is a world of story. This begs the question of the truth and falsity, or the realism and the illusion of our narrative thinking of time. If I say that I see time as a romantic struggle to overcome adversity, what makes that story *real* or *true*?

Are all stories about time true? Can time mean whatever we want it to?

These are natural questions to ask, but answers are not easily found. This is because narratives are not 'propositions' about the world that can be verified by making simple checks against experience. Take two people who both fall ill with the same life-threatening condition. The first sees time in tragic terms and the illness is further evidence that life is a succession of disasters. He becomes depressed and awaits the worst. The second sees time in heroic terms and believes the illness is an obstacle to be overcome. The historical facts in both cases are the same, but the meaning of time for these two people is quite different. We can keep checking the stories against the 'facts', but it will never be possible to say that one is right and the other wrong. These are *interpretations* of the meaning of time and there is not very much point in asking whether one is more 'real' than the other. Both versions account well enough for the 'facts' and as such they are equally 'true'.

That's all very well, but at the individual level some interpretations of time *feel much more real* to us than others. The person who sees time as tragic will really believe this is the truth. And so will the person with an aesthetic or romantic or stoic view of time. We do not think our personal understanding of time is merely as good as all the others. Our personal philosophy of life feels much better, more true and more real than the alternatives. So the view of the world from within our particular time-form is something that we take to be 'true' and 'real' for us in a fairly absolute way.

So the interesting question to ask is why certain narratives work better for us than others. What is the psychological or cultural attraction of one view over the others? What are the advantages and disadvantages of viewing life in this or that way? What do we sacrifice by choosing one narrative and not another? What are the fundamental issues at stake in our narratives of time?

I will argue that our narratives about time are real to the extent that they address our anxiety about the meaning of time. We are drifting in time. The seconds of life are ticking away. We need to know what this passage of moments means for us. Our stories about time work if they can reassure us that time has a positive meaning. In this sense our thinking of time is *redemptive* because it saves us from time-anxiety. The different basic time-forms reassure us in very different ways about the meaning of time. What they all have in common is that they are all real to the extent that they function as redemption histories. In examining a range of basic time forms this book will explore the 'redemptive power' in each mode of thinking about time. This will involve asking how far each time-form can assuage our fear of time, and to what extent our fears remain unresolved.

This is the realism that counts: pragmatic realism. 'Real' narratives are those that 'work' for us by addressing our fundamental concern with time's meaning. Unreal narratives are those that fail to connect with our underlying anxiety about time or merely cover it over with a cosmetic veneer.

Narrative shapes

> History is made while the story is being told;
> it is made in being related.
> > (Jacques Derrida, *Politics of Friendship*)

> Time is like a river made up
> > of the events which happen,
> and its current is strong;
> no sooner does anything appear than it is swept away,
> and another comes in its place,
> and will be swept away too.
> > (Marcus Aurelius *Meditations*)

> The human mind wrote history, and this must read it.
> The Sphinx must solve her own riddle.
> > (Ralph Waldo Emerson, 'History', *Essays*)

It could be argued that the most basic distinction to make in a book on time is the difference between linear and circular time. Popular though it is, this distinction is fairly limited. Circular models of time tend to contain a linear component. The so-called 'cycle' of the seasons, for example, can also be thought of as a repeating line from Spring to Winter. Similarly, linear models of time tend to contain a circular component. So salvation history, often simply called 'linear', may also be understood as a circular return to a lost state of innocence: Heaven the second Eden, Christ the second Adam, Mary the second Eve. The linear arrow of redemption combines with a circular repetition of 'types'. To call salvation history 'linear' tells us something, but by no means everything.

We see the same difficulty with many of the 'classic' theories of history. Karl Marx's revolutionary philosophy of history contains both linear and circular motifs. History moves forward in a line by repeatedly making and destroying epochs (or 'modes of production'). But at the end of the line, history returns full circle to a state of communism first destroyed by the division of labour and the creation of capital. Nietzsche, by contrast, rejects linear history in favour of a circular doctrine of Eternal Return. But a closer look at Nietzsche's writing reveals a linear 'genealogy' of ideas which points towards the 'higher history' of the overman. This is not the place to do it, but similar comments could be made about Vico, Toynbee, Spengler and other proponents of 'circular' history.

So I will not be using the linear/circular distinction as a major analytical tool in this book. By contrast, the shapes that interested me were lines and dots, where dots are 'events' and the lines are the strings of narrative or explanation that connect them up. When we try to understand time from the human point of view, we are generally trying to place the dots into some kind of pattern or sequence. We join them with 'story-lines' that show how the dots relate to one another. Are all the dots on an ascending line heading in some direction? Are they all piling up in a purposeful way? Or are the dots a random splatter, like Rorschach ink blots, scattered here and there without pattern or reason? Or is each dot meaningful in its own right, like the circles on a Damien Hirst spot painting: free-standing events or epiphanies that have their own inherent value? Or perhaps the dots are just an ellipsis in time – dot-dot-dot – a line of events marking time before some future revelation? And how do the events of history, or the events that make up our lives, relate to the 'Big Dot', the event that Christians call the end-time or eschaton? Such are the questions that are thrown up by thinking of time in terms of dots and lines.

I believe that this is the kernel of the human question of time:

what does *this* event in time mean? What lines are connecting this dot with other events in my life or my world? What is the significance of this very dot happening now? Is it a moment of waiting? If so, for what? Is it an episode of work? If so, to what end? Or is this just a beautiful event in itself, something small and perfectly formed, that requires no further explanation? In short, 'what is "now" for?' That's the human problem of time in a nutshell.

In one sense, you don't need a book like this to answer this question, because in all likelihood you will already have a very strong belief about what the events of your life are for. However, it is possible that you have not fully understood your own belief system. You will be operating with some implicit philosophy of time, because it's impossible not to have one. The way you live right now, and your reason for that way of life, are an answer to the question of the meaning of time. But what are you saying about time? What sense if any do you make of the dots of your life? Could you put into words what you think time means, or are you just living it? What do the events of life mean? This book may help to answer that question.

CHAPTER TWO

The Deconstruction of Time

We can measure time, but this gives us no guarantee
that we know what time is.

(Umberto Eco, 'Times')

The clock on the mantelpiece
Has nothing to recommend.

(W. H. Auden, *For the Time Being*)

In thy absence thou dost steere
Me from above.

(Henry Vaughan, 'Content')

What then is time? I know well enough what it is,
provided that nobody asks me . . . 'Time' and 'times' are
words forever on our lips . . . No words could be plainer
or more commonly used. Yet their true meaning is
concealed from us. We have still to find it out.

(St Augustine, *Confessions*)

We need to prepare the ground for the main chapters of this book
by showing how difficult it is to say anything very certain about
time – as St Augustine realised in his *Confessions*. It is also necessary
to show that the unknowability of time is significant, that it is
precisely this *uncertainty* about time – and our *anxiety* and *fear*
about what we do not know – which is the force behind our
philosophies and theology of time and history. We need to be clear
that our thinking about time takes place not only in the *absence*
of definite knowledge, but precisely because knowledge is absent.
Indeed our thinking is *moulded* and *driven* by this absence. The fact
that we do not know the purpose of history – what the past means

or the future holds – provides the energy and spur for the imaginative construction of historical meaning. In the quest for an understanding of time, we are drawn towards mythical pictures and stories of what time might mean.

The idea that our thinking is driven by what we do not know may appear odd, but has a venerable tradition in both sacred and secular writing. In Christianity the 'negative theologians' – the author of *The Cloud of Unknowing*, Meister Eckhart, Angelus Silesius and St John of the Cross, for example – used un-knowing and even the absence of God as the platform for thinking about our relationship with God. Instead of being a problem, *not* knowing God is taken to be a religious virtue, a resource for theological reflection. As Angelus Silesius puts it, the *unknowability* of God is the clearest thing we know about him, and this emptiness of knowledge is the basis for a purer kind of spirituality. We see echoes of this tradition in say, G. K. Chesterton's celebration of the Black Virgin whose dark image 'not clear, not final' draws out devotion; or in Henry Vaughan's vision that within God there is 'a deep but dazzling darkness'; or in Rowan Williams' argument that 'when God's light breaks in on my darkness, the first thing I know is that I *don't* know – and never did.'

In the twentieth century there have been a number of philosophers who have also argued that our thinking is finally determined by what we cannot know. Karl Jaspers suggested for example that our lives are 'illuminated' by so-called 'limit situations' – conflict, suffering, guilt and death – when the security of our knowledge is radically shaken up. It is only when we are aware that there 'is no firm ground under us' that we can understand the meaning of existence. Martin Heidegger argued a similar case, saying that we come to understand time only after we have encountered the unknowable event of our own death. We have to 'crash up' against the emptiness of non-existence – which Heidegger calls 'the Nothing' – and from *this* point work our way back to an understanding of our own lives. However, this insight is by no means obvious. We think that we already understand our own existence because we talk about it all the time. Heidegger disparagingly called our everyday talk about time and human existence 'chit-chat' – all the words are there, but the utterance is detached from a deep personal confrontation with death and nothingness.

13

So we have to break through our ordinary assumptions to grasp the essence of our own lives.

We think we know what time is because we speak about it every day. We successfully make appointments in our diaries. We measure time with astonishing accuracy and we can make time-based predictions about the future. From a practical, day-to-day point of view there does not appear to be any special problem with time. And from this shallow, functional perspective time is indeed relatively unproblematic. But there is much more to time than this. Take the analogy of a TV set. In one sense we all know how a TV 'works' – we press switches and watch the programmes. But if we turn the set around with the back off, how many of us can *then* explain how a TV 'works'? Similarly, we know how to get by in time, how to work with time to get things done. However, it is not so easy to say *what* time is exactly and what it is *for*.

The analogy with the TV set breaks down here because we do in fact have some very definite attitudes about the workings of time. But these attitudes are hidden away in the background of our consciousness in the form of a so-called 'pre-reflective' philosophy. So if you ask people whether they have a philosophy of time, they are likely to say 'no'. In truth though, we all do hold very strong views about time, but these are so imbedded into our thoughts and words that we do not even notice them. Our everyday talk may sometimes sound like idle 'chit-chat', but even our most casual references to time contain profound assumptions about its shape and purpose. Our everyday metaphors of time are freighted with a cargo of philosophical beliefs.

In the last century our metaphors of time were predominantly economic: time was money. We 'spent' time or 'saved' it, 'wasted' it or 'managed' it, 'bought ourselves time' or 'lived on borrowed time', we 'used our time' or even 'killed time'. These metaphors – all comparatively recent inventions – reflected an extreme humanism, the belief that time is somehow 'ours', that we *should* be its masters. This language of mastery, which makes time our instrument is not just chatter, but reflected a powerful enlightenment myth of human power. This view is the one we will later be exploring as 'prophetic time'.

There is nothing 'necessary' about this myth, and human history can show us many alternatives. If we look, for instance, at Shakespeare's metaphors of time we uncover a quite different 'catastrophic' myth of time. For Shakespeare everything is the other way round, and we are slaves who are expended and wasted by time's mastery. We are not in control at all, but head inexorably towards 'the dark backward and abysm of time'. Time is a 'tyrant' who 'leads summer on to hideous winter and confounds him there'. Time is a 'wasteful' and 'bloody' enemy. In the final analysis, we are devoured by the 'tooth of time and razure of oblivion'. Shakespeare's tragic historical view – as we will explore further in a later chapter – pictures human existence as a romantic but doomed struggle against temporal decay. For Shakespeare time is fatal and we are its fatalities.

Beyond both Shakespeare and Modernism, the information age is generating the vocabulary for yet another mythology of time, this time 'kairic' in nature. We are now getting used to a new culture of immediacy and speed. News, information, shopping and services strive towards round-the-clock availability – '24/7', as we now say. Blogging (or weblogging) allows news and opinion to be logged instantly on the Internet without editorial filtering. Bloggers try to capture the spirit of the moment – the latest idea, image, information – and make it available everywhere *now*. Computer 'clock speeds' and 'data transfer speeds' accelerate us towards the ideal of instantaneous response and immediate communication. At the centre of it all is the concept of 'real time'. 'Real time' is the space where things now happen 'live', not just in our locality but globally, so that we can be connected 'in real time' (IRT) – via the Internet, CNN, telephony, messaging – with people and events anywhere in the world. *Big Brother* and other reality TV shows operate on a real-time communication with the audience. Recent TV and film drama – for example *24* and *Phone Booth* – are narrated so that the audience viewer-time corresponds minute-for-minute with the 'real time' of the action on screen. Our lives can be divided between on- and off-line episodes: 'up time' and 'down time'. Our old language is too slow for 'real time' and is being radically contracted into 'textese'. 'Time', for example, is being re-spelled as 'tym' – to avoid any WOT (waste of time). In reaction to this new obsession with immediacy, an artist in the US is constructing 'the clock of the long now' which will run for 10,000 years, ticking once a year and chiming every millennium.

The metaphors of time in any period and in any culture reflect a basic human requirement for myth. What we *know* hardly needs myths. Myths are the thought-form for what *cannot be known*, what must be *imagined*. Mythic constructions are a necessary response to the unknowability of time. Things happen, and they are dispersed in a sequence. But the meaning, pattern and logic of the dispersal of events, the meaning of *happening* itself – this must be narrated. This narration takes place in the most precarious way. The narration of time proceeds in faith over a chasm of unknowing. Our narratives are no more than a prayer that time holds meaning. The possibility that time is meaningless, the possibility of the desolation of time, this is a primary cultural fear. If it works to good effect, the thinking of time works to console us.

The forms of these myths, their types and configurations, their plots, character and purpose are the principal subject of this book. Before examining the various types of time, I need to show more fully why the thinking of time calls for myths. I need to show just how desperately fragile our everyday thinking of time is. To do this I will need to 'deconstruct' some of our familiar assumptions about time. The belief in past, present and future; the belief in the 'flow' of time; the belief that time even exists – all these 'beliefs' need to be exposed as conjectures, creative guesswork and wishful thinking. It should then become apparent that the meaning of our 'lived duration' must be more or less imagined.

Deconstructing time

> Time ... gives us nothing to see.
> It is ... the element of invisibility itself.
> (Jacques Derrida, Given Time)

As we have noted, the unknowability of time is not obvious and we need now to establish just how difficult it is to say what time is and what it is for. We need to examine our key assumptions about time to show how precarious or impossible they are. A concept that will be useful here is the idea of 'deconstruction' – a philosophical term coined in the 1960s by the French philosopher Jacques Derrida. 'Deconstruction' refers to the way in which our fixed ideas have an in-built tendency to fall apart, or 'deconstruct'.

When we think about 'truth' or 'god' or 'reality' we naturally try to make our thoughts as clear and concrete as possible. But often the harder we try to think with clarity, the more muddied our thinking becomes. We may *think* we know what we mean by 'God' (for example), but when pushed to write it down or engage in a serious discussion, our ideas seem less solid, more ambiguous. The reason for this, Derrida argued, is that all thinking takes place using language. And language is an unstable medium, always open to interpretation, always open to *another way* of seeing things.

A key concept in deconstruction is 'undecidability'. Although we *think* that we can *decide* (determine) the nature of 'time' or 'truth' or 'god', these issues are in fact 'undecidable'. In saying this, Derrida is not (as some wrongly believe) discounting the value of words like 'truth' or 'god'. Rather, he is showing that there is an essential uncertainty in these concepts, and that we hold them not as objects of knowledge but faith.

Derrida first applied his theory in the 1960s to show how the idea of time (as set out by the twentieth-century German philosopher Edmund Husserl) 'deconstructs' because we can never clarify what we mean by 'the present moment'. As we try to fix our thoughts on 'the present' it has already gone. Our thoughts and words chase around after 'the present', but it is always just beyond our grasp. So the meaning of our idea of 'the present' is always 'delayed' or 'deferred'. For a while at least – in the 1980s and 90s – Derrida's deconstruction was hailed by many as a revolutionary new philosophy. Certainly Derrida's impact has been very great, but the idea of deconstruction is not so revolutionary.

Whether we go back to the beginnings of Western philosophy or to Christian theology, we find ideas of time being 'deconstructed'. The ancient Greek philosopher Zeno's famous paradoxes of time (as we will see shortly) were an early attempt to show how our ordinary assumptions about time can be used to reach absurd conclusions. St Augustine also breaks off in his *Confessions* to 'deconstruct' the idea of time by showing how our everyday concepts lead to contradictions or nonsense. As we interrogate even the most basic ideas – such as 'past, present and future' or the 'movement' of time – we find that there is little solid ground to stand on. Indeed, there are philosophers and scientists ready with good arguments that time does not exist at all.

17

The upshot of this examination will not be that our talk of time is utterly meaningless or that we know nothing at all about time. The conclusion is rather more ambiguous: we know *very little* about time and many of our basic concepts are confused or vague. For certain, our knowledge of time cannot answer the question of time's shape and purpose. This drives us in a particular direction. Firstly, we realise that we must *imagine* the shape of time in a mythological or narrative way. Secondly, we have little choice but to *trust* time, to have faith in it despite the gaps in our knowledge. Either that or we will despair of time. Despair is always a *possibility* – a possibility that makes faith all the more important.

The division of time

> We speak of time in three ways or modes – the past, present and future. Every child is aware of them, but no wise man has ever penetrated their mystery.
> (Paul Tillich, *The Eternal Now*)

> Time has no divisions to mark its passage; there is never a thunderstorm or blare of trumpets to announce the beginning of a new month or year. Even when a new century begins, it is only we mortals who ring bells and fire off pistols.
> (Thomas Mann, *The Magic Mountain*)

The divisibility of time is one of our most common presuppositions. We think of time as *divisible*, in other words made up of units (minutes, hours, days and so on) or composed of episodes (moments, events, happenings). Our language is telling us all the time that this is true. If I tell you about my day, I will tell a series of stories broken up into episodes: this phone conversation, that meeting, such and such an incident. These episodes can all be allocated slots in the diary. All life is like this. Life feels 'bitty' and we all speak of time as if it were naturally in chunks. Our vocabulary provides resources for us to think in this way and our patterns of thought are ingrained with the belief that time is in parts. The assumption of the divisibility of time is so *fundamental*, so *necessary* for practical existence, that we are not even aware that it is an assumption. And these are potentially the most dangerous kinds of assumptions, the ones that pass themselves off as *facts*.

When I was living in Bethnal Green in London's East End, where eels were a delicacy, I used to see the local fishmonger chopping up live eels for customers. As the eels slithered around, he held one end firmly and chased the body of the eel around the board with his cleaver. The result was an eel sliced up into bite-sized segments ready for cooking. Would it be correct to think that because the fishmonger had successfully divided the eel into sections that the eel therefore really consisted of units? Obviously not. An eel in segments may meet a practical culinary need, but eels are really continuous bodies.

By analogy, time is not *composed* of minutes, hours or indeed any other unit. As Henri Bergson argued, time is a continuous duration. We *impose* calibrations on time – and with good reason (can you imagine trying to live without such divisions?). But the practical necessity of dividing time is not the same thing as saying that time is necessarily divided. Furthermore, the division of time into episodes, events and discrete stories is necessary in order for us to narrate our experience and make sense of what is happening to us. But the narrative requirement that history be divisible does not mean that time itself is given in episodes.

You may object that the division of time is not arbitrary, but is structured by the physical universe: days and years are not human impositions but are determined by the movement of the planets. This is true enough, but a day on Mars lasts roughly 24.6 Earth days, on Pluto a day lasts roughly 6.4 Earth days and a day on Saturn lasts roughly 10 hours and 40 minutes. And none of these various day-lengths is entirely regular. The use of Earth days rather than Mars days is clearly more convenient for Earth residents, but this does not mean that time *really is* composed of Earth days. Astronomically-based time is also always local. The day starts at different times depending where you live and up to the mid-nineteenth century every town kept its own time. The standardisation of time was brought about by social and political agreement, driven by the requirement for a standard national time for the new railways.

Greater accuracy can be achieved with atomic clocks than with astronomical techniques. But just as there are many planets and many days, there are many kinds of atomic clock: caesium, hydrogen and rubidium clocks are based upon quite different atomic oscillations. Caesium 133 atoms are commonly used and their oscillations occur at roughly 9.19 billion times per second. The regularity of caesium oscillations is certainly useful, but it does not tell us anything about time's inherent divisions – if indeed time has any inherent divisions.

But let's suppose for a moment that time really does have inherent divisions. This would create another philosophical problem: how are the divided sections of time connected? This would lead to the presupposition of an undivided primary time-continuum that would hold all the parts of time together. And so we would return to the irresistible conclusion that time is *fundamentally* undivided. We just have to face up to a startling irony: the fact that we can measure the passage of time does not mean that we know anything about time.

The classic 'deconstruction' of the division of time was offered 2300 years ago by Zeno of Elea. Zeno tried to show that the division of time would lead to absurd conclusions. In one of his paradoxes – the athlete in the stadium or progressive dichotomy paradox – Zeno imagines a runner racing a fixed distance from one side of a stadium to the other. Clearly the runner must travel half way across first. So the runner travels half way across the stadium. Then he must run half of the remaining distance. The runner keeps running half the remaining distance to the far side of the stadium, but since he is always halving the time and space between himself and the end, he can never finish the race! Zeno's point is not that it is impossible to cross the stadium (that's a plainly absurd conclusion) but that the divisibility of time is impossible. Zeno believed, like his teacher Parmenides, in the simplicity and unity of the cosmos. Zeno argued this case, with great brio, against the Pythagoreans who believed that everything in the universe was composed of parts.

Zeno's arguments are all very well when we consider the measurable structure of time. But surely time may be divided otherwise, not into units but into the simple and obvious dimensions of past, present and future? Who could argue against that? Although it certainly offends common sense to say that time does not consist of past, present and future, some philosophers do indeed contend that time itself is not tensed. And their arguments are compelling.

The most famous critique of tense was made by the early twentieth-century philosopher J. M. E. McTaggart, who also argued (as we shall see shortly) that time does not exist at all. Think of an event – let's call it M. Before M happens, it is a future event, whilst it is happening it is present and after it happens it is past. This throws up a problem, as McTaggart put it: 'we get a contradiction, since the moments at which M has any one of the three determinations . . . are also moments at which it cannot have that determination.' Take an example: Imagine the event M is you eating an ice cream. M clearly cannot be real in the future because that would leave no ice cream to be eaten when the event happens in the present. You can't have your ice cream in the present and eat it in the future! Furthermore, M cannot happen in the present because there would be no ice cream available to be eaten in the past. And M clearly cannot be past without having previously happened in the present. When considered in each tense, the eating of the ice cream excludes the possibility of the other tenses. The contradiction arises because there is nothing intrinsic to M that makes it past, present or future. M is simply M, it merely *appears* to be past, present or future from a particular perspective. In other words, for McTaggart there are no tensed facts, only tensed perception and tensed language. Even language need not *necessarily* be tensed and it is quite possible to write a novel in the present tense – as for example, Thomas Pynchon does in *Gravity's Rainbow* (for more on this novel, see Chapter Three).

The tenseless view of time has been vigorously contested, recently by the theologian William Lane Craig who argues that there is a strong argument for assuming that our common-sense perception of time as past, present and future actually corresponds with the real structure of time. Applying the American philosopher C. S. Pierce's principle that 'truths, on the average, have a greater tendency to get believed than falsities' Craig can see no good reason for following McTaggart when so much in our experience and use of language confirms our basic belief in tense. In Craig's view it beggars belief that the mass of ordinary humanity should think, act and speak on the basis of past, present and future, but really be deluded.

The arguments to and fro in this debate cannot be discussed here. It is enough for us (as some post-modern philosophers put it) to have 'problematised' the reality of tense – in other words to have recognised but not resolved its ambiguity and complexity. We cannot take for granted our intuitive belief in past, present and future. Astonishing as it may seem, the reality of tense must be *argued for*. But the uncertainty of our knowledge of tense does not stop here. Taking the deconstruction of time along a different axis, looking at each tense in turn, there are further problems with past, present and future. It is to these problems that we now turn.

The curious present

> ... as I pronounce it, this proudly exclusive Now dissolves, flows away and falls into dust ...
>
> (G. W. F. Hegel, *The Philosophy of Nature*)

> The history of the world, is it reduced to the infinitely thin, forever changing, strip of light which forms the Present, wavering between a darkness of the Past which is done and no longer anything at all, and a darkness of the Future, which is also nothing?
>
> (Hermann Lotze, *Metaphysics*)

Of all the concepts used to discuss time, the idea of 'now' or the 'present' is the most pervasive, and with good reason. We feel intuitively that we have a special grasp on time as it happens in the present. The past may be subject to forgetfulness and distortion, the future may be merely hypothetical, but the present feels as though it is 'just there', real and immediate. Although philosophers from Aristotle to Husserl have argued strongly for the idea of the present as the foundation of time, what we mean by the 'present' or 'now' is far from clear.

The idea of the present is in fact so fraught with difficulty that many philosophers eschew the view of the present as some defined unit of time. Some, such as Kierkegaard and Heidegger refer instead to the 'moment': a non-specific interval in which an existential decision must be made. Others, notably Henri Bergson, use the concept of 'duration'. Hegel (quoted above) turns 'Now' on its head, redefining it as an eternal present. We will draw upon some of these concepts in later chapters. For the time being it is enough to examine the difficulty of thinking of time as the occurrence of 'the present'.

One of the first theologians to make a deconstruction of the present was St Augustine in his consideration of God and time in the *Confessions*.

> Of these three divisions of time, then, how can two, the past and the future, *be*, when the past is no longer and the future is not yet? As for the present, if it were always present and never moved on to become the past, it would not be time but eternity. If, therefore, the present is time only by reason of the fact that it moves on to become the past, how can we ever say that the present *is*, when the reason why it *is* is that it is *not to be*? In other words we cannot rightly say that time *is*, except by reason of its impending state of *not being*.

In other words, the present is nothing in itself, but simply the point where the future gives way to the past. Augustine continues his deconstruction with a slightly over-laboured *reductio ad absurdum* of the length of the present. Augustine asks how long the present lasts: is it a century, a year, a month, a day, an hour or a minute? Whichever length we choose, however large or small, the duration of the present can always be reduced. This leads to an inevitable conclusion:

> In fact the only time that can be called present is . . . a point of time as small as this passes so rapidly from the future to the past that it is a duration without length. For if its duration were prolonged it could be divided into past and future. When it is present it has no duration.

So, on this analysis the present shouldn't exist. Augustine repeatedly points out that this conclusion is counter-intuitive. We are apparently aware of the present all the time, and the duration of the present is not an everyday worry. But it is clear at least for our purposes, that the present is a *problem* and that we cannot say easily or precisely what it is.

The complexity of the past

> History would be an excellent thing if only it were true.
> (Leo Tolstoy)

> History: a lucky dip of meanings.
> (Graham Swift, *Waterland*)

> There is no way of telling what yet may become part of history. Perhaps the past is still essentially undiscovered! So many retroactive forces are still needed.
> (Friedrich Nietzsche, *The Gay Science*)

Compared with the fleeting and elusive present, the past may seem to be a more secure dimension. The past seems to be final. We say, 'you can't change the past' and 'what's done is done'. The past appears to be 'dead' and laid out on the slab for examination. Once subjected to philosophical questioning however, the question of what the past *is*, and what it *means*, becomes ever-more complex.

Where *is* the past exactly? I remember going to the Tower of London as a child and returning with a long poster with all the monarchs of England laid out in chronological order. In our everyday thinking, we visualise the past like this – using a spatial metaphor – as though the past is located somewhere behind us, stretched out in an orderly line. Only a few seconds' thought tells us that the past is not located in space, but if not in space then where?

What we mean by the past is some kind of *after-effect* of time's happening – objects, texts, stories, traditions, memories. I remember standing among the ruins of Ephesus and a tour guide saying 'in Ephesus you can see and touch the past'. But the philosopher in me thought 'no, in Ephesus, as everywhere else, you can only see and touch the present.' I can touch the pavements in Ephesus, see the inscriptions, read St Paul's descriptions of past life there. On the basis of this my mind may create a script or images or a 'mental movie' of the past – but all the while I remain stubbornly stuck in current time. The 'feeling' of the past as 'somewhere else' is a trick of the mind. The past takes the form of a set of 'traces' left in the present.

We feel this present quality of the past most clearly, if painfully, in experiences of loss and bereavement. The loss of someone loved is not something gone but a wound in present experience. At least two writers – William Faulkner and Graham Swift – have written novels about history which use stories of bereavement to explore the feeling of the past. In Graham Swift's *Waterland* Mary Crick's present is seared with the loss of a child: she is still 'in the midst of events . . . that haven't ceased. Which it is impossible to get through. Which is why she cannot cross into the safe, sane realm of hindsight.' In an image that runs through the book Swift describes the past as a 'sedimentation' that builds up in the present. William Faulkner's *Requiem for a Nun* centres on the murder of a child. In response to the comment that the child is 'dead', the lawyer Gavin Stevens speaks the line that sums up the novel: 'the past is never dead. It is not even past.' Although the murder is the fulcrum of the story, Faulkner's novel concerns the wider question of US history – bereavement is a special case of the general truth that the past is a dimension of present experience.

It follows that if the past is located in the present, then the meaning of the past is coloured by one's present perspective. The 'traces' of the past are interpreted within the horizon of 'present experience', and what counts as 'present experience' depends who you are, where you are born, the language you speak, your gender, culture and personal history. The past will always appear in numerous versions. Moreover, since the present is always on the move, these versions are being continually rewritten as the past expands and present experience is re-cast. The old adages – 'what's done is done' and 'you can't change the past' – are false. The past is constantly changing, that's in its nature – and it is changing in a countless number of simultaneous versions.

At one time historians dreamed of a final version of history – in the famous words of the great nineteenth-century philosopher of history, Leopold von Ranke, history 'as it really was'. But the complexity of history blocks our path to any single version of what happened. It may at times disturb and frustrate us, but the complexity of the past is a reality that we must live with.

The unknowable future

> Our activity can be directed towards the future only. But the future is completely unknown.
> > (Hans Reichenbach, *The Direction of Time*)

> What we call our future is the shadow which our past throws in front of us.
> > (Marcel Proust, *In Search of Lost Time*)

> Que sera sera, whatever will be will be,
> The future's not ours to see,
> Que sera sera.
> > (Jay Livingston and Ray Evans)

Whatever its complexity we do at least have 'traces' of what's gone before and we can at least *remember* versions of the past. The future, by contrast, leaves no traces or memories. The future is unknown and this has led a number of philosophers – from the ancient Sceptics on – to argue that the future is not real at all. For the future to be real, argued the second-century thinker Sextus Empiricus, it would have in some sense to be 'present'. But if it were present it would not be in the future.

These (and others like them) are rather obvious arguments and do not unsettle our conviction that the future – as what *will be* our present reality – is of immense importance to us. The future is the dimension of consequence. We act in the present, but the present does not contain the outcome of our actions. Our present actions play themselves out in times to come. Since consequences are always futural, the future is also the dimension of ethical responsibility. We may be responsible *for* the past, but we cannot be responsible *to* the past. It is the future that will sooner or later hold us to account.

There are immense ethical problems here. How can we act responsibly when we cannot calculate the outcome of our actions? Our own lives and human history are full of well-intentioned mistakes. One ethical response – so-called 'deontological' ethics (or ethics of duty) – is to ignore the future and simply do 'the right thing' whatever the imagined consequences. The alternative

– 'consequentialist' ethics – is to try to second-guess the future, planning present actions by calculating their probable outcome. We will see in the coming chapters how this ethical difference shows up in the models that we use for historical understanding. (A and K type time both incline towards the deontological view; whereas P type time is essentially consequentialist.) The point being made is that the future raises in us a problem of ethical action – either pushing us back upon timeless moral principles, or inviting us to predict future events.

The essential unknowability of the future demonstrates very well both the general problem that we face with time and the way that this problem calls for mythical thinking – because the future must be thought in the imagination or else not thought at all. Further-more, the imagination of the future is crucial to the construction of an overall model of time. Whether in ancient prophetic and apocalyptic literature, or in modern science fiction, the imagin-ation of the future is a way of thinking through the goal of human history, its ends and purposes.

One of the ironies about our thinking of the unknown future is that it must draw its materials from what we already know. As Northrop Frye puts it, 'we know nothing of the future except by analogy with the past.' And the past, as we have seen is really a dimension of the present. Thus all the tenses of time converge on the present. Yet, as we now also realise, the present is all but impossible to determine. The result? Splendid confusion.

The arrow of time

> Life can only be understood backwards.
> But . . . it must be lived forwards.
>
> (Søren Kierkegaard, *Journals*, 1843)

> Ch-ch-changes,
> pretty soon you're gonna get a little older.
> Time may change me
> but I can't trace time.   (David Bowie, 'Changes')

> Time is like a river made up of the events which happen,
> and its current is strong; no sooner does anything

appear than it is swept away, and another comes in its
place, and will be swept away too.

(Marcus Aurelius, *Meditations*)

There are difficulties, clearly, with our ideas of tense. But these
notwithstanding the three dimensions of time do at the very least
appear to have an absolutely fixed order. We seem to move *from*
past *to* future in the direction of 'time's arrow'. Everything in our
experience appears to confirm the one-way flow of time. Life seems
to proceed forwards with yesterday always behind and tomorrow
always ahead. I cannot remember the future and I cannot bring
about events in the past. I cannot keep promises in the past and
having made a cup of white coffee it is not possible to rewind my
actions, tip the milk back out and drink it black. The flow of time
appears to be identical with a mono-directional process of change
and entropy: eggs become chickens; we all get older and not
younger; the universe gets steadily more disordered, and Humpty-
Dumpty cannot be put back together again. Even if time travel
were possible we would surely feel that we were either going with
or against the natural flow of time. We may think, intuitively that
time *must* flow, but even this basic assumption is a problem. And
it is not just a sophistic problem for philosophers: Einstein did not
believe in the so-called 'arrow of time' and according to a 2002
survey in *Physics World*, only 43 per cent of physicists think that
the direction of time is real.

Part of the difficulty lies with the assumption of time's 'flow'.
Picture yourself standing by a river. From your fixed position you
can observe the water flowing past. That's because you are
stationary and the water moves relative to you. Now transfer the
analogy to time. If time is, as the hymn says, 'an ever-rolling
stream' then where is the bank from which we can observe its
flow? Surely we are all within time and there is no platform outside
time to stand and see whether time flows or not. Indeed if we
imagine a god-like point-of-view from which we could see all
history at a single glance, time would look perhaps not so much
like a stream as a static system. There would be no implicit direction to this system, just a sequence of events, which could be read
off as easily in either direction as A-to-Z or Z-to-A.

We may object that 'flow' is just a metaphor and that what we really mean is that time is change. If nothing changed we could not be aware of time, it would feel (if we could feel it) as though time had stopped. This is all very well, but the idea of time as change would work both forwards and in reverse, as the philosopher Michael Dummett argues in his classic essay 'Bringing about the Past'. As observers in a backwards world – with apples shooting from the ground to attach themselves to the branches of trees – we would not be able to *explain* what was happening, and we would not know *how to act* in such a world, but a reversed world would still *look like* a world of change and time. Martin Amis depicts this brilliantly in *Time's Arrow,* a novel narrated backwards in time. We can still follow the story Amis tells, even though every causal link is wired in reverse.

The feeling of the direction of time is given, then, not so much by *change* as by our ideas of *causality,* that's to say *how* things change or *the relation* between things that change. We can tell the difference between our world and a reverse world precisely because apples fall from branches and not vice-versa. Moreover, I can intend an action one minute and realise it the next. But I cannot apparently act retrospectively. Having said this, Dummett argues that it is not necessarily *irrational* to think that we can act retrospectively and some physicists argue for the possibility of alternative universes in which time would go the other way.

If causal connections are the same thing as the 'direction' of time, can we then say where this direction is pointing. Is time going 'forwards'? If so, where is 'forwards'? We customarily depict 'forwards' as a movement from left to right, or a clockwise rotation. But couldn't 'forwards' *just as reasonably* be said to be a right to left movement? Wouldn't clocks work *just as well* going anticlockwise with the numbers reversed? Could time not, *with just as much meaning*, be said to be going 'upwards' or 'to the left'? Isn't the idea of time's direction – like so many of our ideas of time – just a *metaphor*? These metaphors are only natural and 'make sense' to us because they emerge from our experience of the world. We are human so, instinctively, we depict time in terms of the human body. Time 'marches' forward, just as we walk through the world. The future is 'ahead' and the past 'behind'. What could be more natural, but ultimately more deceptive, than this metaphor of time's 'forward' direction?

Although we may 'feel' that we are facing forwards in the passage of time, it would perhaps be a better metaphor to picture ourselves with our backs to the future. We cannot see the future, so what we have before our eyes is the present with its traces from the past. The future is coming from where we cannot see – from behind. We are constantly dealing with what time delivers over our shoulders into the present. All the time our spatial metaphors are giving us to think we are looking 'forwards', our faculties of understanding are working in reverse – working back from present events to piece together an idea of what is happening. As Kierkegaard observed, we would do best to think of time having not one but two metaphorical arrows: life lived forwards and life understood backwards.

The possible non-existence of time

> Nothing really changes. And nothing is really in time.
> (J. M. E. McTaggart, *The Nature of Existence*)

> It was not in the past, nor shall it be, since it is now, all at once, one, continuous.
> (Parmenides)

> Time is an illusion. Lunchtime doubly so.
> (Douglas Adams, *The Hitchhiker's Guide to the Galaxy*)

By way of a final 'deconstruction' we need to consider the question of the very existence of time. Bizarre as it may seem there are some good reasons for thinking that time does not exist. Parmenides of Elea denied the reality of time and St Augustine hinted at this possibility, by putting in doubt the existence of past, present and future. But Augustine was really just exploring his perplexity with time, rather than making a proper argument for its non-existence.

The remarkable seventeenth-century Jewish philosopher Spinoza made the case in a more persuasive fashion. Spinoza – who is often regarded as a pantheist – believed that everything in the universe at all points in time was a series of modifications of one single reality. Imagine a person from Mars finding himself in a 70s disco, seeing all around him strange squares of light drifting across the walls. Because he cannot see the mirror ball on the ceiling, he assumes that the light patterns are separate entities. In fact, the apparently independent squares of light are modified versions of the mirror tiles on the ball. From the embodied human vantage-point we can only comprehend the world in small episodes spaced out in history. So time only appears within a restricted 'mode of thinking'. To know what the world is *really* like we need to see things *sub specie aeternitatis* or from the perspective of eternity. From this point of view, time does not exist, and what we call human history is laid out like an immaculate architect's model: A place for everything and everything in its place. 'To understand it in its totality, under the aspect of eternity, is also to know that everything in the world exists by necessity, and that it could not be other than it is.' But how do we square the non-existence of time with our everyday experience that things really are happening? Spinoza's argument is that the perception of time arises from inadequate knowledge. Since (Spinoza argues) our intellect is not bound in time we can use our reason and intuition to obtain what he called an 'adequate' idea of reality. So we can at one and the same be living and acting 'in time' at the same time as knowing that it doesn't really exist!

Not convinced? Think of human history as a novel. Whilst we are reading the novel we are 'inside' the story, turning the pages, seeing events unfold. Reading feels like a 'flow', some events lie behind, others ahead and we appear to be moving along with the current of the narration. But when we have finished the book, the flow stops, the 'time' of the story ends. Now we can contemplate history as a single completed work, *sub specie aeternitatis*. You may object that there is no 'outside' to time, that we are not so much readers of the novel as characters trapped inside, perhaps *everything* is inside time. Quite. However, we can at least *imagine* a view beyond time. Kurt Vonnegut does this in *Slaughterhouse 5*, when he imagines the inhabitants of the fictional planet Tralfamadore. 'The Tralfamadorians can look at all the different moments just as we can look at a stretch of the Rocky Mountains, for instance. They can see how permanent all the moments are, and they can look at any moment that interests them. It is just an illusion we have here on Earth that one moment follows another one, like beads on a string.'

The best known modern argument against the existence of time was offered by J. M. E McTaggart in 1908. We have seen already how McTaggart argues that thinking of events as past, present and future (which he calls the 'A series') leads to contradictions. We may object, however, that even if they are not *tensed,* events are still *sequenced* in an order – a, b, c, d, etc. – running from 'earlier' through to 'later'. McTaggart calls this sequence the 'B series'. But nothing changes in the B series, everything has a fixed place in the sequence. So, argued McTaggart, the B series is not a time-series at all, but a static list: 'Whenever we perceive anything in time – which is the only way in which, in our present experience, we do perceive things – we are perceiving it more or less as it really is not.'

These arguments are important to us, not in order to dislodge our belief that time is 'there' for us as an everyday reality, but in order to expose the mystery and uncertainty of our everyday reality. The nature of time simply cannot be taken as read. The question of time is radically open, as the poet Geoffrey Hill memorably puts it: 'history stands, a blank instant, awaiting your reply'.

Time-anxiety and the need for myth

> Nowhere is mythology more alive than in historiography.
>
> (Mircea Eliade, *Myth and Reality*)

> Time is of your own making,
> Its clock ticks in your head.
> The moment you stop thought
> Time too stops dead.
>
> (Angelus Silesius, *The Cherubinic Wanderer*)

So much for the deconstruction of some of our concepts of time. Where does this negative approach leave us, except standing among the ruins of some well-loved everyday assumptions? The deconstruction of time has shown us something important, necessary and essentially positive: that our ideas of time have an uncertain and ambiguous basis. Since time does not furnish us with a ready-made meaning, this meaning must be constructed. We put together the meaning of time not as a hobby but as a pressing life necessity. The absence of an inherent meaning to time is not just an intellectual curiosity: it *worries* us. The 'existentialist' philosophers had special terms for this worry: anxiety or dread. For example, Kierkegaard said that we experience anxiety as a kind of dizziness or vertigo as we become aware of the sheer scope of our human freedom. The meaning of life has not been 'given' but lies before us as a 'terrifying' range of possibilities.

Martin Amis captures this anxiety in his short story 'The Time Disease'. Amis imagines the year 2020 when 'time-anxiety' has become a cultural illness. Everyone carries mirrors to check for signs of 'coming down with time'. The only antidote is to stave off time with boredom or bore others by 'going on and on about anything that enters our heads'. This is a culture that has lost any sense of time's meaning, which has forgotten how to think of the future. Time is no longer hopeful or expectant, but a wasting illness. With no consoling myths of redemption, everyone is exposed to time-anxiety, which acts like a cultural virus.

Time-anxiety is more than a simple fear of death, although the fear of death is one form of time-anxiety. Time-anxiety is a fear about *life*: a ball of fear in the gut as we are gripped by the horrific realisation that human existence may possibly be a form of living death or a meaningless parade of events. Since our lives have no natural meaning in time, at the back of our minds is an awareness that time may, after all, just be pointless – as Shakespeare put it a 'tale told by an idiot, full of sound and fury, signifying nothing'. Naturally we recoil from this possibility and seek consolation in meaningful versions of time: myths that tell us that 'all will be well', that the tale is not idiotic but sublime and full of significance, myths that explain how meaning can be seized from the flux of experience. So our myths about time are not arbitrary, but derive from our fear that time may be meaningless. And this fear is not irrational but derives in turn from our very real uncertainty about the concept of time.

Let us take a closer look at what is meant by 'myth'. When we try to describe the events that happen in time, we naturally begin to write history. We list events, connect one event with another, and give shape to events and to time. But what kind of activity is the writing of 'history'? One of the debates that have dogged the philosophy of history is precisely the question of the nature of historical study. Is history a kind of science, like the natural sciences, that uses 'data' (historical traces) to describe the past in purely objective terms? Or is history a creative process, more like literature, of writing plausible stories about the past? Or perhaps history is a so-called 'human science', akin to sociology, that aims to show the underlying laws of human behaviour and structures of human organisation?

We cannot launch into this debate without a lengthy detour. Clearly there are important issues of objective truth in history. But history does not come pre-packaged as an objective story. To become intelligible, history must be *narrated*. So Paul Ricoeur concludes his three-volume study of history and narrative, saying that the historian must become a story-teller. Without this story-telling ability history would be a bald chronicle of events, a tedious catalogue of everything that happened. The story-teller must decide which are the key events, the key people, the key historical forces and explain how these combine. To use the current jargon, history must be *emplotted*, that is to say given a narrative form.

What I am calling 'myth' is the underlying structure or form that we give to time and history. Depending upon our mythic outlook, the passage of time can be narrated in quite different ways. A trivial example would be the difference between the pessimist and the optimist: The former expects the passing of time to be endlessly disappointing; the latter sees time as providential. Both have prefigured the tale of life with a mythic expectation. Take as another example the history of the twentieth century. Is the history of the last century a tale of human achievement, with new technologies and unprecedented social improvements? Or is it a tragedy of human pride, scarred by genocide, nuclear weapons and ecological disaster? It all depends upon one's mythic pre-disposition: Do we subscribe to the myth that humanity is engaged in a heroic struggle to build its own future? Or do we believe the myth that humanity is fatally flawed and that only a God can save us? This is just an illustration, and it is true that things are never this black and white. But when we tell the story of human time or even the story of our own lives, we do make a mythic choice and impose a particular pattern upon events. Until recently the history of the West was in the balance between two grand ideological myths of history: First, the Marxian myth that productive forces were driving history in a revolutionary process towards an ideal future. Secondly, the capitalist myth of the benevolence of the free market. The capitalist myth has now become our new orthodoxy. But for how long? George Soros, the capitalist guru, has recently written about 'the imminent disintegration of the global capitalist system'. So watch this space.

The myths that govern our thinking of time, as with any other narrative, can be analysed by genre. Someone who has attempted such an analysis is Hayden White, an American philosopher of history, who in 1973 wrote a ground-breaking book called *Metahistory*. In *Metahistory* White attempted to produce an exhaustive classification of historical genres, arguing that the historical imagination falls into four basic categories or 'modes': romance, tragedy, satire and comedy. When we look at time from a *meta*-historical perspective the details of history fade away and the deep patterns of history emerge. White called these patterns 'modes of historical emplotment'. To these modes of emplotment, White added four 'modes of explanation' and four 'modes of ideological implication'. The result was a grid of genres, which could map out the different styles in which history is narrated. In this way White tried to tease out the deep grammar of our historical imagination, or in other words the mythological structures of history.

White's brilliant *Metahistory* is perhaps the finest example of what has become known as the 'narrativist' approach to history. However, White's study has its shortcomings. First, White's analysis restricted itself strictly to the writings of classic theorists of history: Nietzsche, Ranke, Burckhardt, Marx and so on. This was a necessary academic focus, but White's classification might also be extended beyond academic history to classify the way that we all imagine the history of our own lives, individually and culturally. Secondly, White failed to explain why we commit ourselves to this or that mode of understanding. (What is the attraction of the tragic view? Why choose to narrate history as romance?) He offered no *psychology* of the historical imagination.

This book also offers a 'metahistorical' classification of the 'historical imagination' in terms of the myths we tell ourselves about time. But unlike White's metahistory, I will attempt to classify the ways (we are calling them 'types of time') in which we think about time in ordinary life and culture. Furthermore, we will try to show both the *psychological appeal* of different types of time, and the *psychological motivation* (I have called this 'time-anxiety') that impels us to mythologise human history. It is to the foundations of that time-anxiety in the catastrophic type of time that we now turn our attention.

CHAPTER THREE

Catastrophic (or C type) Time

Time devours all things.

(Ovid)

Change and decay in all around I see.

(H. F. Lyte, 'Abide with me')

The wan moon is setting ayont the white wave,
And Time is setting with me, O!

(Robert Burns)

Nothing 'gainst Time's scythe can make defense.

(Shakespeare, 'Sonnet XII')

'Can I do anything?'
'No! All is trouble, adversity and suffering!'

(Thomas Hardy, *Jude the Obscure*)

The representations of time

We do not *know* what time is, but we *fear* what it may be. Time may be pointless and this prospect makes us anxious, haunting life with the possibility of ruin. This fear becomes visible in our various cultural symbols of time. Wherever we look we find time depicted in images of waste, exhaustion, expenditure, dissipation, termination and loss. We mostly keep time-anxiety in check. But scratch the surface and it's there. Our cultural representations of time betray an inner fear, an unconscious worry that time adds up to nothing.

At the centre of our time-anxiety stands the figure of Kronos (or Saturn), according to Hesiod 'the most terrible' of the ancient Greek Titans and the so-called 'Father of Time'. Having heard in a prophecy that he would be overthrown by his own son, Kronos ate his own children before they could usurp him. Kronos was paranoid about time and its fatal possibilities, paranoid to the extent of consuming the objects of his anxiety. As a result Kronos/ Saturn became the figurehead of death and destruction, presiding over the natural cycles of decay and regeneration. His symbol was the scythe, an indiscriminate blade that razes all to the ground. Small wonder that the ancient astrologers saw those under the sign of Saturn as 'saturnine': gloomy, phlegmatic and depressed.

It is perhaps with Kronos that time was first seen as *consumptive* – as Ovid put it a 'devouring' time that eats up life. In Western folk-mythology Kronos appears as the Grim Reaper, a hooded skeleton carrying weapons: either his scythe to harvest souls *en masse*, or an arrow to slay an individual victim. Sometimes Kronos is carrying a clock, sometimes an hourglass, sometimes a sealed letter. He may also be carrying a coffin or a spade. Sometimes he appears with wings as an 'angel of death', at others he is a decomposing corpse. In all his various forms, the skeletal Kronos has become our standard cultural symbol of time, appearing frequently on funeral monuments and clocks. There is an excellent public example on a clock now standing in the main dome of the Victoria and Albert Museum in London: Kronos is shown with scythe and hourglass and the word IRREVOCABLE is printed in Latin between the numerals on the clock-face. Arguably the most famous and intriguing of Kronos' representations is as the leader of the so-called *Danse Macabre* or *Totentanz*. Here Kronos is a carnivalesque but sinister figure of seduction, either beckoning us to join him in death, or violently bringing death upon us. The *Danse Macabre* is disturbing because it hints at a collusion between humanity and the corruption of time, an issue that I will consider later in this chapter.

The figure of Kronos has been taken up in various ways by poets and novelists. In *Jude the Obscure* Thomas Hardy memorably depicted Time as a sickly child. 'Little Father Time' is the nickname of Jude's son and he performs a symbolic function in the novel, referencing Jude's personal misfortune to the possibility of tragedy on the cosmic scale. Critics generally agree that Hardy's use of a mythic figure of Time in a realist narrative does not work all that well, but it certainly makes an impact. When Little Father Time

hangs not only himself but Jude's other children few readers will
not be horrified: this is one of the bleakest episodes in nineteenth-
century fiction. Little Father Time's curse is that he cannot be
consoled with the transitory joys of life: even 'laughing comes
from misapprehension'. He gazes 'over some great Atlantic of Time'
and can find no meaning in it. Despairing of the future, he concludes that the world would be better with fewer children. Hardy's
echo of the infanticide in the Kronos myth is surely deliberate,
and perhaps more cruel than the original story. Kronos' infanticide
was eventually stopped by the trickery of his wife Rhea, who sub-
stituted a stone for Zeus the youngest of his children. Kronos ate
the stone instead, and Zeus survived to force his father to dis-
gorge the other children. Hardy's novel is more obviously
catastrophic. Nothing at all is salvaged from Little Father Time's
tragedy. *Jude the Obscure* is a myth about the absence of historical
meaning, a story of human existence in a malevolent universe.
This was Hardy's last novel, written in 1895 when a number of
writers – Joseph Conrad and Oscar Wilde for example – were connecting the *fin de siècle* with a tragic view of culture and theories
of historical decline. As the doctor attending the deaths observes,
Little Father Time represents 'boys of a sort unknown in the last
generation – the outcome of new views of life. They seem to see
all its terrors before they have the staying power to resist them.'
Little Father Time is an emblem of *fin de siècle* pessimism, tragedy
unfolding at the heart of what should be new life, a fresh age born
not into hope, but a sense of fatal degeneration.

   In our own time, Ted Hughes has appropriated the figure of
Kronos in his *Crow* poems. The ancient mythologies allowed their
protagonists to change form, and Kronos also took the form of a
crow. The skeletal Kronos is sometimes shown with a crow flying
overhead or perched on a nearby branch. As a consequence, the
crow has become a symbol of ill fate and impending catastrophe –
in Edgar Allan Poe's famous words, the 'grim, ungainly, ghastly,
gaunt and ominous bird of yore'. Hughes casts Crow as the violent,
dissolute, indestructible hero of an alternative creation myth.

> God tried to teach Crow how to talk
> 'Love' said God. 'Say, Love.'
> Crow gaped, and the white shark crashed into the sea

> And went rolling downwards, discovering its own
>   depth.

Crow represents history's other potentiality: time heading to oblivion. Whereas in the biblical creation story, time is redeemed by love, in Hughes' dark myth, Crow triumphs over humanity, over the scorching sun, even over death. God is shown powerless to stop Crow's advance. Crow's time, the consumptive energy of Kronos, is our worst fear: the possibility of the meaninglessness of it all, the anxiety that time adds up to nothing: the empty hourglass, a snuffed candle.

We see the Kronos myth echoed in almost all representations of time. The running of rivers, the trickling sands of the hourglass, the 'winds of change', the cruel wheel of fortune, the washing of the tide, the funeral bell and the dwindling candle – everywhere we look time is represented as loss and exhaustion. Another ancient Greek depiction showed time as pure self-consumption: Uroboros, the mythical snake that feeds on its own tail. In some Christian writings Uroboros has been seen as an emblem of sinful humanity: history feasting endlessly on its own errors. In his painting 'The Triumph of Death' Pieter Brueghel combines in one image a terrifying range of fatal time symbols. There is a candle burning down in the foreground, on the horizon smoke drifts away in the wind. Everywhere Kronos – in the form of industrious skeletons – is busy gathering in his harvest. Boats, carts and nets are carrying the ill-fated to their destiny. Wheels of fate spin on axles in empty space and a bell tolls the passage of time. Brueghel's picture is a panoramic vision of the Kronos myth: time as pure, unreserved consumption. Brueghel's attitude is symptomatic of the fear written into all Western symbolism of time: it is hard to think of any symbol of time that implies generosity, increase, growth or providence. Except perhaps the sun and the sundial.

Even the ticking of a clock has a negative cultural meaning: time is 'ticking *away*', we say. In literature, film and television, the sound of a clock ticking is a standard way of signalling that time is running out. The countdown of a clock, often some kind of time-bomb, is a stock-in-trade cinematic method of narrating impending doom. The action cuts back and forth between the time-bomb and the hero's 'race against time' to stop it. The device is not always used so crudely. Ridley Scott, for example, has employed the 'clock countdown motif' to powerful and complex effect in *Blade Runner* (1982). Rutger Hauer plays the role of Roy Batty, a Nexus 6 'replicant' with a four-year artificial life-time. The film is set in a future America that Scott describes in the script as 'Hades'. The hours of Batty's life tick away pointlessly as he struggles to understand his existence and searches out his creator. Ultimately, minutes before his own death, Batty creates the meaning of his life by saving Deckard (Harrison Ford) from falling to his death. But even as Batty expires, Ridley Scott leaves the question of the ultimate meaning of time wide open:

> BATTY
> I've seen things you people wouldn't believe.
> Attack ships on fire off the shoulder of Orion.
> I watched c-beams, glitter in the dark near Tannhauser
> Gate.
> All those . . . moments will be lost . . . in time . . . like
> tears . . . in rain.
> Time . . . to die.

Batty's dying words express the sigh of time's transience, the possibility of the sheer waste of it all. They are beautiful words that remind me of a similar sentiment in the famous lines of Thomas Nash four hundred years earlier:

> Brightness falls from the air
> Queens have died young and fair
> Dust hath closed Helen's eye.

Life can feel like pure descent, a long slow drop through time, a shower of dust glittering in the dark.

It is easy to see how the consumptive view of time chimes with ordinary experience: age seems to enfeeble and destroy us. It feels as if time is a kind of decay, corroding life, freshness, youth and innocence. Time appears to play cruel games with us, granting life with one hand and snatching it back with the other. I can still vividly recall the first time I sat with someone who was dying. Mary clasped my hand as if to hang on to time. And when it was over, the prayers said and respects paid, time felt empty and I wondered seriously about the point of it all. When something as critical as death cracks through the shell of our habitual existence, time can feel like pure loss. The Romanian theologian Mircea Eliade has called this feeling the experience of 'profane time'. Eliade argued that a 'terror of history' underlies the human consciousness of time. We are engaged, he argues, in a 'struggle against Time, the hope to be freed from the weight of "dead time", of the Time that crushes and kills'. Eliade defined profane time as time devoid of purpose, form and structure. Mere theories of time are not potent enough to protect us from the terror of history. Only religious faith and practice has the power, argued Eliade, to invoke a 'sacred history' that can expunge 'profane time'.

This 'profane' view of time as a sudden or drawn out process of dissipation or ruin is what I am calling the Catastrophic type of time. Now, as in ancient times, the vision of the utter meaninglessness of history is a view from which we still violently recoil. The Catastrophic mode – the imagination of time as dissolution, decay and oblivion – has had a vast effect upon modern consciousness. Whether it is the Holocaust, the spectre of nuclear disaster, the fear that we will destroy the planet through greed, or that meteors will smash the planet to smithereens, a primal anxiety – for moderns and ancients alike – is that history will either add up to nothing or at least nothing but annihilation. The absence of redemption and meaning is the defining feature of C time, and this is why it is not to be confused with apocalypse. An apocalypse may be a terrible event, but it at least gives meaning to history. In Greek the word 'apocalypse' literally means 'revelation'. For example, the flood was 'apocalyptic' because it clarified God's moral indignation and opened the possibility of a fresh start to history. But 'catastrophe' means 'ruin', a spoilation without meaning, or any fresh start. Time in the Catastrophic mode is quite simply pointless.

C time is not just an idea but can all too easily be an everyday experience, for example in clinical depression. As the psychiatrist Henri Ey observed, a person's attitude to time is a key feature of depression. In the depressed state, the time of life has no rationale and everything appears to conspire against happiness. The C type world feels dark, empty, terrifying. Nothing has a purpose, nothing gives hope, nothing is beautiful. For the depressed person time has no goal, it unfolds meaninglessly, cruelly, fatally. And it does so without relief. However, C time is not just a psychological state, it also repeatedly sears into life to become an historical reality. We do not have to look far into recent history to find episodes of genocide, torture, famine and disease. These remind us that barbarism and abstract suffering are constant human possibilities, constant risks. As we gaze upon history we surely share occasionally the anxiety of the depressive. Perhaps human history is *fundamentally* barbaric. Perhaps C time is not just a feature, but the defining feature of life. And from this fear we are repulsed in search of historical meaning: for purpose, hope and beauty.

The C type in Christianity

> What is crooked cannot be made straight.
>
> (Ecclesiastes 1:15)

> Man wastes away like a rotten thing
> Like a garment that is moth-eaten.
>
> (Job 13:28)

> Time is the passing of a shadow.
>
> (Wisdom 2:5)

> Where to turn without turning
> to stone? From the one side
> history's Medusa stares,
> from the other one love
> on its cross.
>
> (R. S. Thomas, 'Where?')

The Christian story of salvation is the story of an error that must be overcome in history. In the Garden of Eden human time gets off on the wrong foot – a crime is committed against God and thereafter humanity is condemned to repeat itself in endless moral mistakes. The fall instigates a C type history of original sin that humanity cannot undo. A positive history can never start because each new generation is born into the same error. C type history is a tragic game with no exits.

The remedy for this is a new narrative of redemption: the arrival

43

of a messiah who will allow time to unfold without error. With the incarnation he enters history, born in time, to shift its course, to open the possibility of an escape from the vicious circle of C type time. The redemption narrative defines itself against C type time; it is C type time that requires, that begs for redemption to occur. The resurrection is the ultimate overcoming of C time – the derailing of what St Paul calls the 'old order of sin and death' – to create the possibility of a redemptive history, virtuous time that works itself out positively.

The Bible represents C time in a variety of metaphors and images. In the Old Testament, notably in the Psalms, the threat of C time is everywhere in the shape of pits of corruption, waste and desolate places, the valley of the shadow of death, the pollution of idols, the defilement of sanctuaries, wicked enemies with evil hearts and unclean lips and a wind of change that blows us away like grass. The prophets speak of history overrun by chaotic and meaningless processes of nature: 'briar and thorn', nettles and thistles. Isaiah, for example, likens the world to a wild-growing vineyard (Isaiah 5:1–4). In the book of Job, time flees like a shadow, and wastes away like a river that wears down stone (Job 14). In the New Testament, the most vivid image of C time is the fate of the 'Gadarene swine'. Jesus is confronted by a group of demons and casts them into a herd of pigs. The pigs succumb to a violent C impulse and immediately destroy themselves by leaping from a cliff into the sea. In Luke's version the word used instead of 'sea' is 'abyss', a term for the primal ocean or world of the dead. In Greek the word 'a-byss' literally means 'without bottom', a space without ground or depth. In the abyss one would be in an eternal state of falling. This is a mythic tale: the Gadarene swine suffer metaphysical horror rather than a literal death. If we can imagine it without absurdity, those pigs should still be thought of in free-fall now, forever caught in the pull of C type gravity.

St Paul theologises profane time as the 'corruption' of the created organic order. The decay of organic matter is a natural metaphor for C time. Everything in nature tends towards decay, as William Blake evokes in his poem 'The Rose':

O Rose, thou art sick
The invisible worm

That flies in the night,
In the howling storm,

Has found out thy bed
Of crimson joy:
And his dark secret love
Does thy life destroy.

Matthew's Gospel in particular depicts C time in terms of decomposition. Those caught in C time are represented as rotting fish (Matthew 13:47), decaying fruit (Matthew 7:17), or decayed corpses in whitewashed tombs (Matthew 23:27). Our experience as embodied beings appears to confirm the presence of C time as organic decay. The passage of time correlates with physical debility and we can almost 'feel' the pull of C time with physical ageing. The feeling of bodily deterioration is all the more heightened by the sense of growth in wisdom with age. St Paul argues that our souls merely inhabit a 'tent' of flesh, which will be 'swallowed up by life'. Although 'our outer nature is wasting away, our inner nature is being renewed day by day' (2 Corinthians 4:16). Time seems to run in two directions at once: the body follows C time to oblivion while the 'soul' presses forward in wisdom. We 'wither into the truth' as Yeats put it, 'fastened to a dying animal'.

But, as Paul explains, this is just the backdrop. The physical process of corruption will be reversed by Christ. In 'the twinkling of an eye', the gears of C time will be thrown into reverse. Those who have died will not continue to rot away, but will be raised 'incorruptible' as new bodies fit for heaven. The question of how C time can be reversed has been a topic for serious theology, for example in John Donne's Easter Day sermon on 're-compacted bodies'. 'The dead body' says Donne 'falls by putrefaction into a dissolution, into atoms and grains of dust'. But the decomposed body undergoes a process of 're-efformation' (re-structuring) so that the fragments are 're-compacted' to produce a refurbished body for the soul in heaven. In a passage that seems ludicrous now, Donne wonders about the technical problem facing God in reconstructing a decomposed body. The body would become food for worms and grass. The grass in turn would become food for cows, and the cows food for humans. Over time each body would end up dispersed along food-chains leading in countless directions. How would God manage to reverse all these processes? Simple, said Donne: God has special cabinets in which to collect the disparate components of each body!

The redemptive reversal of corruption is echoed in the eucharistic redemption of eating and drinking. Eating and drinking are seen as aspects of participation in the consumptive operation of time. The eating of an apple, the inaugural sin, makes eating an emblem of all sinfulness. They ate and drank in the decadent days before the flood (Matthew 24:38). Worrying about food and drink, Jesus tells us in the Sermon on the Mount, is a distraction from the kingdom (Matthew 6:31–2). In Hieronymous Bosch's triptych, 'The Garden of Earthly Delights', we see a panoramic vision of the corruption of eating. The left panel shows the Garden of Eden. Adam and Eve wait serenely with Christ by the tree of knowledge while animals at their feet represent normal consumption: a bird eats a frog, a cat drags away a mouse. In the central panel we see a world in which human consumption has become licentious: everyone is madly eating fruit, fruit hangs in the air, lies on the ground, floats in the water and dangles over open mouths. In the right panel we see Hell. Here consumption has become anarchic gluttony: devils and monsters gorging on the bodies of the damned. The passage of time follows the line of eye as we read the triptych from left to right – first paradise, then the world, then hell – humanity feasting itself into oblivion. It's hard to enjoy lunch after seeing this picture. Bosch's baroque vision of moral decomposition is far from being a relic of a lost culture. Damien Hirst's installation 'The Impossiblity of Death in the Mind of One Living', presents catastrophic time literally, as a rotting head consumed by flies.

However, one of the first things that people notice about Jesus is that, unlike John the Baptist, he 'comes eating and drinking'. The other St John, the Evangelist, places the marriage feast at Cana at the very beginning of his Gospel, the first 'sign' of Christ's identity. The transformation of vast quantities of water into wine signals the reality of an alternative order of consumption. Christ's kingdom is depicted everywhere in metaphors of food and drink: water, wine, fish, lamb, figs, grapes, corn, mustard, herbs, salt, leavened and unleavened bread. The fulfilment of this kingdom will be a banquet, a complete trouncing of consumptive time. The Eucharist – a foretaste of the feast to come – is virtuous consumption. Jesus enters time not to condemn it, but to consecrate it, to redeem the time. His resurrection is a reversal of organic decay and is accompanied by meals at Emmaus and the Sea of Tiberias.

Although Jesus comes with the glad tidings of redemption, he also intensifies the awareness of C time with warnings about damnation, grinding of teeth and everlasting fire. What is more, Jesus' teaching gives the threat of C time a new and frightening twist: C time may be coming from *within*: unfolding in our own heads, in our selfish thoughts and desires. To think something ill, says Jesus, is as bad as actually doing it. And defilement does not travel from outside to inside, from flesh to spirit, but in the other direction. We are not safe anywhere, not even in our own thoughts. All this serves to remind us of what we already know in our heart of hearts – that C time is an ever-present danger: Our lives are suspended in meaning by a thread of redemptive narrative, as R. S. Thomas puts it 'a rope over an unfathomable abyss'. Profane time is always a *possibility*. It is always *possible* that we will open our eyes one morning to stare at the disenchantment of time, no longer knowing what time is for or why we are living it.

The issue of time is super-intensified during the passion narrative. Having shown little regard for chronology, allowing months and years to pass without note, the gospel narratives suddenly become preoccupied with questions of timing. Jesus says that 'after two days the Passover is coming' (Matthew 26:2) and he will be arrested and that his resurrection will be after three days. Peter's betrayal is prophesied to occur at the precise timing of the cock's crow. Jesus' second period of prayer at Gethsemane lasts an hour. Jesus' sentencing takes place at 'the sixth hour' (John 19:14). His cry 'My God, my God why have you forsaken me' takes place at 'at the ninth hour' (Mark 15:34). The precise moment of Jesus' final breath is indicated in all four gospels. The confrontation with time is suddenly brought into sharp focus, fixing the reader's gaze evermore tightly upon the hinge between catastrophe and redemption. In the crucifixion Christ collides with C time in an ultimate catastrophe: the death of God. As the hinge of time turns, the resurrection reverses the catastrophic event of the crucifixion. Jesus' body, which should be decomposing in the tomb, is in fact confounding the physical processes of decay. Whether the resurrection happened is beside the point, at this juncture. The resurrection narrative is depicting the beginning of an alternative redemptive mode of *time*. Redemptive time will be the very opposite of catastrophic degeneration.

If Christ is the romantic hero who snatches time from the jaws of catastrophe, Judas is the tragic hero – the Macbeth of the gospels – who colludes with C time and goes down with it. The Bible doesn't say what happened to Judas after his death, but tradition sketches in the lurid details. Dante, on his imaginative journey through Hell, sees Judas before him being attacked by Lucifer:

> 'That soul who suffers most of all'
> My guide explained 'is Judas Iscariot:
> the one with head inside and legs out kicking.'

As the worst sinner, Judas was thought to deserve the worst punishment. Some have found this vicious, vindictive idea of hell too much to stomach. Matthew Arnold, for example, recalls a 'more humane' legend in his poem 'St Brandan'. Once a year, on Christmas Day, Christ would release Judas from the eternal fires of Hell and permit him to soothe himself on an iceberg. Wagner's Flying Dutchman is another who lives in a mitigated hell: the Dutchman is cursed to sail the seas for eternity, unless redeemed by love (which of course happens). But hard-line conceptions of *absolute* hell do not allow for the redemption of catastrophic time – not even on Christmas Day. Hell is the attempt to picture C type time in its final outcome. And time is crucial to the conception of hell – whether it is Sartre's hell of other people locked in a room for eternity or the sulphurous furnace that is never extinguished. The point is that there is no remission, no days off, no get-out-of-jail-free card. Remission – however distant – would be hope. But as Dante observed, the damned must 'abandon all hope'.

If anyone were to attempt to develop a thoroughgoing C type theology, it would have to involve the radical absence, failure or perversity of God. Having said that, the contemplation of C type time is seen as a necessary Christian discipline. *Momenti mori* – symbols of death such as a human skull – were important reminders of the reality of earthly corruption. A popular pre-modern image was of 'the three living and the three dead'. The image shows three cadavers delivering a cautionary religious message to three people still alive: This is your fate, so mend your ways now! Christianity also taught the importance of training for death in advance, the *ars morendi* or 'art of dying', so that the soul was prepared to meet its maker. In liturgies too, attention is paid to corruptive time. On Ash Wednesday, for example, the priest draws a cross in ash on the worshippers' foreheads saying 'know you are dust and to dust you shall return'. In this way Christians are invited to focus upon the ruin of time in order to emphasise the need for redemptive history. As Thomas Merton put it in his book *Contemplative Prayer*, 'unless the Christian participates to some degree in the dread, the sense of loss, the anguish, the dereliction and the destruction of the Crucified, he cannot really enter into the mystery of the liturgy.' This, says Merton, puts the Christian in a 'kind of hell', but it is 'a hell of mercy and not of wrath' allowing us to 'escape the cage of emptiness, despair, dread and sin'.

We find an elaborate example of Christian contemplation of C type time in Edward Young's series of *Night Thoughts on Life, Death and Immortality* originally published between 1742 and 1745. Together, Young's nine 'night thoughts' constitute a long theological poem on the theme of time. Young's work is not well known now, but the poem enjoyed great popularity throughout Europe in the late eighteenth and early nineteenth centuries. Young meditates at length upon the corruption of time, allowing himself to confront head on the possibility of a universe working on C type time. William Blake – who was commissioned to illustrate the poem in 1795 – distils the essence of Young's meditation in the personification of Time as a grotesque humanoid figure. The point of this meditation is to lead the mind 'through various scenes of life and death and from each scene the noblest truths inspire'. Young's journey through darkness is intended to bring into relief the beauty of redemption, as Young says, 'gold glitters most where virtue shines no more, as stars from absent suns still have leave to shine.'

In the coming chapters, we will examine the Apocalyptic, Kairic and Prophetic responses to C type time. These however, are all alternatives to the C-type view. Before looking at these alternatives, we need to ask whether there are any ethical possibilities *within* the C type view of time? Is it possible, at one and the same time, to believe in the inevitable deterioration of life, *and* to believe that human choices and actions have some significance?

The ethics of attrition

> . . . All in war with Time for love of you . . .
> (Shakespeare, 'Sonnet XV')

> The fateful question for the human species seems to me to be whether and to what extent their cultural development will succeed in mastering the disturbance of their communal life by the human instinct of aggression and self-destruction.
> (Sigmund Freud, *Civilisation and its Discontents*)

> In the dark times
> Will there also be singing?
> Yes, there will also be singing
> About the dark times.
> (Bertolt Brecht, 'In the Dark Times')

The idea that time *consumes* us, quickly or slowly, until it has eaten us away in death is a common view in secular art and literature. Shakespeare provides perhaps the best example. Shakespeare's view of time is not consistent, but the exploration of C type time is a feature of much of his work. The sonnets – which are obsessed with the C type – see life as a war against time, a day-by-day catastrophe that destroys all human endeavours. Time is a thief who steals life from us, an ogre controlling our destiny, a parasite sapping our vitality and purpose, and in the end the assassin that destroys us. This view is presupposed in the tragedies where the heroes struggle against latent historical forces: Macbeth's collusion with a supernatural destiny; Romeo and Juliet, thwarted by 'a greater power than we can contradict'; the 'decay' that follows Lear's 'sad steps'; Othello's suicide ('no way but this, killing myself') or Hamlet, the vain humanist, who finds himself spiritually power-less to act against the 'corruption' of the Danish court. Even in the comedies – where the plots eventually unwind to good effect – the protagonists are generally servants rather than masters of their destinies. The comic plots tend to tie everyone into a knot of confusion, which is suddenly untangled for a happy ending. The underlying presupposition is that time is a trickster who 'makes and unfolds error' for our amusement.

What Shakespeare describes in dramatic terms is our everyday human feeling of time-weariness, the 'petty pace' that creeps on until the 'last syllable of recorded time'. It's Murphy's Law writ large: what can go wrong will go wrong and at the worst possible time. When one door opens, another one slams in your face. One outcome of this could be the default of ethics: self-pity, fatalism, cynicism and apathy. However, Shakespeare responds robustly to the problem of time with a romantic ethic of valour and endurance. Against the tragic C type backdrop we must battle to keep faith and to find love, beauty and goodness. Our dignity lies in trying to snatch back fragments or 'scraps' of time's meaning – despite the fact that time will get us in the end, and the fragments of meaning will be blown away. Within such a strong C type outlook, one can only adopt a 'de-ontological' ethic of virtue. With time as a 'universal wolf' that even devours itself, ethics clearly cannot secure itself in achievements: there is little point in making plans that will simply be swept away, as Ulysses points out in *Troilus and Cressida*:

> . . . Time hath my lord,
> A wallet at his back, wherein he puts
> Alms for oblivion, a great-sized monster
> Of ingratitudes. Those scraps are good deeds past,
> Which are devoured as fast as they are made.

Since 'disasters grow in the veins of actions highest rear'd', Shakespeare looks to duty as the source of ethics. Time may twist our actions to bad effect, but it cannot stop us doing our duty. We can at least 'persevere' doing 'the right thing', faithful to the end, even as 'envious and culminating Time' sweeps our efforts away. There is some consolation here: it is, at least, better to have loved and lost.

The time of Shakespearean drama is redemptive in one harsh and minimal way: it does at least bring out the truth. Time exposes lies, hypocrisy, betrayals, falsehoods and occasionally love. Truth, as ancient wisdom taught, is the daughter of time. The pressure of time cracks the casing of human affairs to reveal what has really been happening. A delayed or hidden letter – like the letters sometimes carried by Kronos – is a popular device for the arrival of the truth: Friar Laurence's letter to Romeo; Goneril's letter of betrayal; the hidden letters at the end of *Othello*. Time eventually brings enlightenment to the confused, the deluded and perplexed. But the timing of truth can be cruel. The truth pushes Othello over the brink. Friar Laurence's letter arrives too late to stop the double suicide of Romeo and then of Juliet. Laurence's letter does turn up and the truth does come out, but it provides no consolation. Time's revelation of truth is sometimes expensive and often extortionate.

Shakespeare's ethic of trust and endurance is most evident in a host of female protagonists – Cordelia, Imogen, Julia, Miranda, Perdita, Katherine, Desdemona, Juliet – who remain faithful despite suffering, betrayals, separations, humiliations and cruelty. Virtue is won by remaining constant against the vicissitudes of history and human fallibility. Faithfulness eventually restores broken relationships, even if (as often happens) they are swiftly snatched away by death. This is meagre compensation for the damage time inflicts. But faith and virtue are precious, and we find ourselves leaving even the darkest of Shakespeare's plays with a powerful sense of the value of life. Something in us warms to the romance of lost causes. Even a failed struggle against time can inspire us to face life more valiantly. Somehow, Shakespeare manages to dignify the war with time, making us heroic in defeat: 'Golden lads and girls all must, / As chimney-sweepers, come to dust.' After the nobility and romance of the human struggle, life in the end is just powder, and it may not even glisten as it falls.

We see a modern, more ironic version of the ethic of attrition in the work of the American novelist Thomas Pynchon. Pynchon's sprawling, nearly unreadable, book *Gravity's Rainbow* opens with the sound of rocket screaming across the sky. The rocket symbolises the human longing to rise above the given circumstances of life, as one protagonist puts it: 'I want to break out – to leave this cycle of infection and death. I want to be taken in love: so that you and I, and death, and life, will be gathered inseparable, into the radiance of what we would become.' Pynchon brilliantly and chaotically shows C time as an absurd succession of pointless endeavours and meaningless coincidences. The plot of the novel, like the plot of life, really tells us nothing of ultimate significance; it is simply the process of 'rolling-stock absence, of maturing rust'. We may long for something more than catastrophe, but Pynchon shows our hopes falling from the sky – 'the ascent will be betrayed by Gravity' – and the rocket plummets into a packed cinema. The novel ends only a second away from a catastrophic explosion. Pynchon allows only the slightest shred of hope: 'There is time, if you need the comfort, to touch the person next to you, or to reach between your own cold legs.' Shakespeare at least leaves us with the warm glow of human heroism. Pynchon provides no such consolation. His characters are staunchly non-heroic – their combat with time has no dignity and ends in disaster.

Sigmund Freud offers a more optimistic struggle with C time. The nineteenth century ended, it's often said, in 1914. Sigmund Freud was, like all of his generation, horrified by the destructiveness of the First World War. That war dealt a massive blow to the Enlightenment belief that European history was progressing towards a more civilised future. And Freud, after seeing the horrors of mass warfare, tried to develop a secular, pseudo-scientific theory of the C tendency. How do we account for the aggression within humans, their capacity both for killing and, in certain circumstances, their apparent willingness to be killed? Writing of the First World War, Freud said: 'think of the excess of brutality, cruelty and mendacity that has spread itself across the civilised world.' Can we believe that 'only a handful of unscrupulous and ambitious men' are responsible for 'loosing all these evil spirits? Were the millions of the led not partly guilty too?' What puzzled Freud was the apparent human *desire* for self-destruction, a perverse longing for catastrophe. Freud speculated that within each of us are urges (drives) that provide the psychological energy for human life. One is the life drive, the other is the 'death drive': *eros* and *thanatos*. The death drive leads us towards aggression and self-destruction. With this two-drive theory, Freud was able to understand the battle with the Catastrophic mode of time as more equal. The death drive is not a fateful force that we can never overcome, but a structurally flawed part of our nature that we can at least try to keep in check.

In the 1930s Albert Einstein challenged Freud in a letter to explain the human propensity for evil and asked: 'Is it possible to control man's mental evolution so as to make him proof against the psychoses of hate and destructiveness?' In his reply to Einstein, Freud tells us to use the life-instinct against the death instinct: to build 'emotional ties' between people, a 'community of feeling'. We must pitch life against death, not just externally at the cultural or national level, but internally and individually we must seek life over death. We are conflicted between a longing for life and a drive to destroy life: Freud saw civilisation caught in 'a continuous struggle between love and the death drive'. But Freud gives us hope that although we can never defeat *thanatos*, we can at least hold out against it over time. We can at least stop catastrophe happening, even if we cannot eradicate the catastrophic impulse.

At the end of his letter to Einstein, Freud adds an interesting comment, he writes that 'there is no need for Psychoanalysis to be ashamed to speak of *love* in this connection, for religion uses the same words: "love thy neighbour as thyself".' Freud admits that at a certain point our rational scientific languages cannot cope with what is happening to us and we must turn to art or religion. As Freud puts it succinctly elsewhere: 'every science comes to an end in mythology'.

The ethics of unmasking complicity

> Is there some deviant logic unfolding more powerful
> than that provided by reason?
>
> (J. G. Ballard, preface to *Crash*)

One of the disturbing features of Freud's view is that it implies a built-in human complicity with the catastrophic impulse. The exploration of our collusion with destructiveness was one of the central concerns of the twentieth-century French thinker Georges Bataille. Bataille believed that we should understand both evil itself and our complicity with evil. He was intrigued by writers who had made evil their theme, for example, the notorious Marquis de Sade. Before he is misunderstood, it is worth saying that Bataille was nauseated and repulsed by the writings of de Sade and he described de Sade's occupation as 'enumerating to the point of exhaustion the possibilities of destroying human beings, of destroying them and of enjoying the thought of their death and suffering'. Yet Bataille regarded de Sade as 'a genius'. What Bataille found admirable in de Sade was the psychological thoroughness of his investigation of evil. De Sade's world is the exact opposite of 'civilised' Western society which tends to shield its eyes from evil, offended (and rightly so) by the C type impulse. In Bataille's view it is important, in the cause of self-understanding, to give voice to 'those uncontrollable desires, on the negation of which consciousness has based the social structure and the very image of man'. De Sade's positive contribution was in making evil *visible*.

One of Bataille's observations is that evil is not static, but an entropic reality that acts itself out in time. Bataille wrote of de Sade that 'the language of *The One Hundred and Twenty Days of Sodom* is that of a universe which degrades gradually and systematically, which tortures and destroys the totality of beings which it presents.' In other words de Sade articulates a no-holds-barred version of the C type myth. The question that Bataille poses for us is how far we, as 'civilised' people, are removed from the catastrophic consciousness of time. This question, Bataille implies, has an ethical value in its own right.

In his study of Hegel, Bataille tries to show how a destructive-sacrificial logic, of destroying 'this' to achieve 'that', is essential to our ideas of enlightenment progress. Yet this sacrificial logic, depending as it does upon destruction in the name of a higher good, is not so far from a C type logic of dissolution which destroys for its own sake. Bataille's point is that we cannot crisply separate P and C time; Catastrophe exists within Prophetic time as part of its structure. Thus even in our noblest acts, we are complicit with '[the] tooth of time which kills incessantly and is incessantly killed'.

In the chapter on Prophetic time I will return to the idea that all human efforts at civilisation are contaminated with *some other impulse*. Who can look at the history of the last century and not wonder in horror at what we have done? We do not have to be unduly cynical to wonder whether all human efforts at progress are doomed and whether time, after all, is not really Catastrophic. The reality of our fear of C time is still powerful. And because this *fear* is powerful, so is our need of powerful myths of time's meaning.

Yet for all our fearfulness, C time may not be real at all. As we have seen in Chapter Two, time has no given meaning. Perhaps the apparent cruelty and horror of history can be explained away as part of some greater meaning and beauty. Perhaps we are simply too close up to time to see the panoramic truth of its providence. St Augustine thought this. He said that evil was not real but just the absence of good. There is no 'death drive' for Augustine, just the absence of a life drive. *Perhaps*. Until we can eliminate that 'perhaps', anxiety of C time will remain all too real.

C phobia

> 'Twas grace that taught my heart to fear,
> and grace my fears relieved.
> > (John Newton, 'Amazing Grace')

> When man faces the tragic
> He liberates himself from it.
> > (Karl Jaspers, *Tragedy is not Enough*)

> The great majority of so-called Christian populations continue, down to our day, to preserve themselves from history by ignoring it.
> > (Mircea Eliade, *Cosmos and History*)

Having set out now some of the features of C time, let us turn to look at the sense in which *fear* of C time is real for us. I have said that the Catastrophic mode is the most 'real' of the types of time, but how can this be justified?

We need to be clear that time is only *possibly* Catastrophic: it is *open* to the C type interpretation. There is evidence, plenty of evidence, to support the belief that time is really Catastrophic. But it is not *necessarily* so. However, since time *can* be understood in the C type mode, our *fear* of C is real and it is the reality of our C phobia that drives our positive and redemptive thinking of history. You may already be champing at the bit with objections, and I will be looking at one major objection shortly. For the time being, let us stay with the idea of C phobia.

The kind of reality we are talking about is analogous to the 'reality' exercised in Freudian theory by repressed thoughts, feelings and memories. From the point of view of conscious life, it

looks as though we are operating on the basis of deliberate inten-
tions, feelings and concrete entities. But this does not take account
of our repressed material – messy, symbolic and latent – that is
determining the way in which we operate consciously. The ideas
and feelings we repress are those that we cannot bear to have in
our conscious thoughts or in our conventional memory. So things
that are repressed get hidden away and encrypted in symbols and
myths. In our dream consciousness, repressed memories may
surface, but often in mythic structures that require interpretation.
Hence Freud's interest in Oedipal and other kinds of myth which
operate in the background of conventional daily life.

I do not want to draw the analogy too closely. (I do not want,
for instance to have to posit the idea of something like 'a cultural
unconscious'.) But the idea of repression does provide a helpful
image of how the fear of C time operates in a hidden but all-too-
real way behind our manifest narratives of redemption. We would
not need the 'real' story of redemption unless there were a 'real'
human concern about the reality of catastrophe.

But when I say that C phobia is 'real', this 'reality' is of a very
strange kind. C phobia is not the same as the real fear we might
experience facing some concrete danger such as a diagnosed illness –
we could address that fear in a practical way. C phobia is the
abstract fear of the *possibility* that the whole of life is some kind of
sickness. It is *metaphysical* fear: the fear of an unbearable *idea*. The
C idea is also strangely *empty*, because it could take any number
of forms. C phobia is not fear of a *specific* catastrophe, but of
catastrophe in general. C time is a hollowed-out idea, the shell
of an idea, the space where an idea *could* be, but *is not*. C time gets
defined ultimately by a series of negatives: time with *no* purpose,
no meaning, *no* revelation, *no* hope.

Recently the philosopher Slavoj Žižek has used the metaphor of
'haunting' to describe how latent cultural fear plays itself out in
modern life. Žižek has spoken about the function of 'spectral
history' in relation to our post-war cultural understanding of
Europe. Žižek sees the Holocaust as the clearest modern example
of 'spectral history'. It is not the 'real' Holocaust that has power
over us, but the fear or ghost of the Holocaust that haunts, or
should haunt, the modern imagination. Žižek suggests that the
Holocaust was 'too traumatic to be integrated into historical

memory'. Yet despite this, the ghost of the Holocaust determines our modern thinking about human nature, historical progress, and political organisation. We could say that C time functions as a general 'spectral history'.

Our redemptive narratives should save us from the reality of C type time in two ways: first, they should supply us with a positive model of happening that permits us to structure our existence in a pleasing and hopeful way; and secondly, they should help us to deal with our anxiety about the catastrophic potentialities of time. In other words successful religion should supply *real* hope and *real* comfort. So the 'reality' of our religious life relates directly to the 'reality' of C phobia. This is not to say that the reality of redemptive narrative is *derivative*, but that it is *locked into* the possibility of the reality of C. Remove C phobia and there really is no need for a redemption narrative at all. That would be paradise and we are not there yet.

Religion is not always successful in dealing with C phobia. Often religion can contribute to the repression of our fears. As we have seen from the consideration of the biblical depiction of C type time, redemption takes place as a direct engagement and reversal of the corruption of time. An effective Christianity needs to work similarly, not smothering our fears with happy reassurances but engaging with our fears in a way that acknowledges the connection between C anxiety and redemptive narrative. Yet Christianity can often be a mechanism that presents redemption in the form of a repression of anxiety. Reassurances that 'God loves you' or the much-quoted phrase from Julian of Norwich that 'all will be well', are empty unless they connect with the catastrophic sub-narrative. 'God loves you' is only a powerful thought in the face of a universe that is possibly devoid of love; 'all will be well' is only reassuring when locked-in to the fear that all may be catastrophic. Many people find this connection with C uncomfortable: they do not like to hear psalms that urge violence on our enemies, or the hard sayings of Jesus, or talk of hell. But redemption does not mean very much unless we acknowledge that there is some need for it.

There are, of course, plenty of perverse versions of Christianity where the preaching of C type time is used manipulatively as a motivational technique to encourage converts: 'join us or you go to hell'. This form of Christianity is really Manichean because it sees time divided 50/50 between redemption and catastrophe, God's time and the Devil's. It encourages C phobia for the most cynical of reasons: ecclesial power and control. It not only asserts the reality of C phobia but asserts the reality of the C mode of time itself. It can never rid itself of this collusion with the Catastrophic mode of time.

Other forms of Christianity can give the appearance of dealing with C type time, while really using images of catastrophe to conceal C phobia. An obsessional interest in Good Friday and the sufferings of Christ may appear to indicate a lack of repression of C phobia. But this can be what has been called 'repressive desublimation', that is to say the presentation of tame objects of fear in a way that effects an even more deep-seated repression. We see this with the millions of images of the crucifix that are hung on walls or around necks as a talisman. The crucifix apparently reminds us of the torture and death of Christ. But in truth the image works to disengage us from the reality of suffering, to wish it away in the most superstitious fashion. We see the same thing everywhere in our 'liberated' popular culture. Blood-soaked horror films, for example, appear to cater for an audience ready to face the possibility of catastrophe. In reality they are a form of escapism. Sexual images used in advertising would appear to speak to a sexually liberated culture, but in fact keep sexuality stuck in a safe repertoire of stereotypical and politically naïve symbols.

An effective Christianity manages to assert a positive, redemptive view of time in a way that acknowledges C phobia without affirming it. This kind of Christianity can converse openly and therapeutically about suffering and death, about guilt, shame, doubt, theological uncertainty and moral ambiguity. It can continue these discussions against the backdrop of faith in a redemptive view of time, but without feeling the need always to short-circuit the conversation back to dogmatic assurances about time's meaning and purpose. This is a Christianity that can contemplate the catastrophic consciousness and not be overcome by it. To redeem something is not to obliterate it, or hide it, or hold it down. Redemption – in the biblical sense – is a metaphor of ransom, and means to 'liberate'. This is the very reverse of repression. An effective Christianity liberates by uncovering the reality of our anxiety. This need not be depressing. The experience

of even the bleakest of Shakespeare's tragedies can be deeply cath-
artic and uplifting. This is because Shakespeare dares to speak about
our fear of catastrophe, and puts us in touch with our profound
concern with the redemption of time. An effective Christianity
needs to be just as honest.

A question of trust

> Faith is the assurance of things hoped for,
> The conviction of things not seen.
>
> (Hebrews 11:1)

I said earlier that there is an objection that we need to discuss. We
may agree that the C type of time is a feature of experience. But
we may also balk at the idea that fear of catastrophe is the starting
point for the production of redemptive narrative. Isn't this rather
negative? Isn't our experience of time basically one of *trust*? We
trust time to bring us benefits. We *trust* that in life we will find
beauty, love, goodness. Fear is what happens when *trust* breaks
down or wears thin. Surely it is *trust* in divinely-created time that
is the basic religious attitude. In our relationship with God we are
in receipt of *promises* that we *can* trust. These *promises* are the basis
of religious reality.

These are warm sentiments, but they disguise the fact that trust
has a sub-structure. Trust is indeed a basic religious attitude. But
trust is always a response to something else. Trust is required
because we have uncovered gaps in credibility, faith or knowledge.
If beatitude and providence were obvious we would simply *know*
them as everyday truths. I do not have to trust that my hand is
attached to my wrist – it's just there and saying that I 'trust' it to
be there would be meaningless. I do not have to *trust* that there
are three sides to a triangle. But I do have to trust other people,
because their goodwill is not guaranteed. In fact there are plenty
of people of ill will. Similarly, the benevolence of time is not a
'fact' but something that I trust despite contradictory evidence and
despite my complete lack of knowledge of the future. We need to
trust because time does not always look like a blessing, because it
is *open* to the C-type interpretation. As the New Testament teaches,

trust/faith fills in the spaces where we cannot see. So trust always assumes a situation that calls for trust.

Christianity has always assumed the existence of basic human needs which have not yet been met: needs for forgiveness, salvation, love and so on. These needs (or other needs) must come first otherwise religion loses its rationale. The simple truth is that Christianity is all about salvation. And salvation only makes sense if we are being saved *from* something. The attempt to begin theology from the given benevolence of history will do Christianity out of a job. The fact is that the benevolence of the world is *radically uncertain*: that is why it can only be grasped in faith and trust.

Matthew Fox's popular book *Original Blessing*, tried to argue the opposite case – that authentic Christianity is not about salvation at all, but about affirming the blessing of a creation that has already been given to us. He says that we need a *Via Positiva* – a theology of primal affirmation. Yet even as he recommends a creation spirituality of trust, Matthew Fox introduces a version of the very salvation history that he condemns. It is the *Via Positiva*, he says, that will *save* us from the previous errors of Christianity. Fox argues that Christianity cannot be trusted, that it has 'failed people in the West' for 'six centuries' and is now in need of *rescue*. As a result of 'negative' spirituality we are, Fox argues, 'assaulting our land' and 'assaulting our bodies' and we 'deeply require an earthly spirituality'. If Western Christianity cannot adopt his *Via Positiva* Fox says that we are 'clearly doomed'. Fox certainly tries to write the salvation story in a different way – there are many ways to narrate salvation – but his is nonetheless a theology of redemption. We cannot avoid the fact that Christianity is either in the salvation business or not really in business at all.

Trust is central to Christian experience. But we must not forget why trust is necessary. The possibility of the existence of Catastrophic time forces us down one of two paths – either into despair, or into a radical act of trust in the redemptive potential of history. This act of trust can be inflected in quite different ways – as waiting, being and working – and this inflection produces quite different modes of Christian practice. Having now considered *why* trust is a necessary religious response, let us look at *how* this trust plays itself

61

out in the three redemptive models of time: Apocalypse, Kairos and Prophecy.

CHAPTER FOUR

Apocalyptic (or A type) Time

Introduction

> Someday you will find me
> Caught beneath the landslide
> In a champagne supernova in the sky.
>
> (Oasis, 'Champagne Supernova')

> Surely some revelation is at hand.
>
> (W. B. Yeats, 'The Second Coming')

> The darkest of enigmas, human hope
>
> (Edward Young, *Night Thoughts*)

The traffic lights are red and you are waiting in your car. You know that the green light will appear soon. Your mind and body are poised in readiness for this event. You have one hand prepared to release the handbrake and a foot covering the clutch. Your eyes are tilted up towards the lights, which blink from red to green. This is your permission to shift from one mode of time to another: you may now exit 'waiting time' and cross into 'progressive time'. You release the handbrake and away you go. Daily life is made up of hundreds of such time-shifts: routine gear changes in and out of 'waiting'. These shifts are so commonplace we hardly notice just how much waiting we do.

Notwithstanding the occasional red light and traffic jam, time in the car is generally progressive, pushing onwards towards a destination – after all, we call it *driving*. Every street we pass, every junction we cross is another step towards our goal. But every so often another kind of time interrupts the driven progress of our journey: progress stops and we are forced to wait. This waiting time contains no task, has no given meaning and contributes nothing to our main purpose. We simply have to endure this waiting time, either serenely or drumming our fingers in frustration on the wheel.

Waiting time is everywhere in our lives. I conducted a rough audit today and counted two hours of waiting time: from waiting for the kettle to boil (one minute) to waiting for someone who was late for our meeting (twenty-five minutes). If I live to be seventy-five, I will have spent six years and three months of my life just waiting – that's 8.5 per cent of my existence! If we could have all our waiting time in planned blocks, then perhaps we could do something with it. But waiting often just appears in scraps here and there, unscheduled, making it almost impossible to *use*.

The vast majority of us see waiting as a waste of time – wouldn't you rather be travelling than just hanging around? Society uses enforced waiting as a method of punishment. A prison sentence is punitive waiting. The teacher who asks a naughty child to stand against the wall during break-time is using waiting as a penalty. The person who can force another to wait has a particular power. Indeed, keeping others waiting can be a way of 'showing them who's boss'. Very few of us will regard waiting time as a positive opportunity, we generally avoid it if we can, and resent waiting if it is imposed on us. Waiting feels like 'dead time', the very opposite of living, purposeful existence.

But waiting needn't be like this. I remember a particularly long wait at a train station in Mexico. I was travelling from Mexico City back to the United States via Guadalajara. At Guadalajara I changed platforms and sat down to wait for a connecting train that was due in a few minutes. Fifteen minutes passed and I asked when the train would arrive. 'Soon' was the answer. Indeed 'soon' continued to be the answer whenever I asked. Ten hours later I was still waiting, having given up hope of the train ever arriving. But my mood had passed from frustration to acceptance. By the end I was enjoying the waiting: observing, chatting, doodling, strolling. There was something refreshing about waiting time. I seemed to find in myself an inner patience that felt fundamentally good. Ironically there seemed to be *more* meaning and peacefulness in time that had no purpose.

These times spent waiting for 'something to happen' are what I am calling Apocalyptic or A type time. In its broadest sense, the apocalyptic consciousness is an expectant openness to what life may bring. Although rooted in theological ideas of time, the apocalyptic consciousness is as alive in secular thought as it is in theology. The best known example of secular apocalyptic thinking is arguably Samuel Beckett's *Waiting for Godot*. *Waiting for Godot* is an analysis of waiting for a revelation that never happens and may never happen. The characters fill up the time of the play with diversions, crazy pastimes, and preparations for the arrival of Godot. The awaited apocalypse – which goes under the name 'Godot' – is not specifically Christian (Beckett was irritated by Christian interpretations of the play), but a more general, non-religious longing for 'something' significant to happen.

Apocalyptic time – for St Paul as much as Samuel Beckett – takes place as watching, hoping and waiting for a future revelation. Whether that revelation ever comes is beside the point. What's important is that revelation is *expected*, and this expectation shapes an entire attitude to time and existence. Apocalyptic time is pregnant time, time orientated towards a disclosure to come. The receptive emptiness of Apocalyptic waiting feels quite different from the Kairic celebration of the present moment, or the driven pace of Prophetic time. Beckett captures brilliantly the texture of time in abeyance. The reason that we recognise the truth of Beckett's depiction is because we spend much of our own existence in the Apocalyptic mode.

There is room for confusion here because in common modern usage the word 'apocalypse' is used in a negative sense. In everyday speech we use 'apocalypse' to mean destruction on the grand scale. Hence Francis Ford Coppola's *Apocalypse Now* (1979) is a depiction of the dark cruelty at the heart of modern warfare. However, I am using the word 'apocalypse' in its literal Greek meaning of 'revelation', or 'uncovering' (specifically in the sense of pulling back a veil). A meaningless and destructive end to history is covered in this book by the term 'catastrophe'. The distinction is important because the Apocalyptic view of history is in fact *positive*: it believes that the truth of history will sooner or later be revealed. The Catastrophic view on the other hand sees time as a senseless expenditure of energy culminating in disaster or dissipation. The absence of any revelation (apocalypse) is the key feature of Catastrophic time. By contrast, the hope or expectation of revelation is precisely what makes time *apocalyptic*.

In the Apocalyptic view (by contrast with the P type) the goal of history is unknown. When, why and how history will end is not within our control. What will be is 'God's business' or 'fate' or 'chance' or 'sod's law' or 'a turn up for the books'. For the person working in Apocalyptic time, the idea of 'working towards the future' would seem pointless. It is equally pointless from the vantage point of the present to try to second guess the outcome of the future. The logic of history is not available to us, so A type time is 'non-rational' in the sense that it is impossible to work out the reasoning behind the apocalypse.

To be within A type time is to be present at a vigil. A type time promotes an ethic of waiting, of individual vigilance and preparation. This chapter will argue that the A type church is primarily concerned with individual moral and spiritual purity. Every action must be correct in itself because history may not last long enough, or be known clearly enough, to justify a means–end pragmatism.

From prophecy to apocalypse

'Prophecy! What's the good of thinking what will be!' He raised his glass. 'To the destruction of what is,' he said calmly.

(Joseph Conrad, *The Secret Agent*)

Yet saints their watch are keeping
Their cry goes up 'how long?'
(S. S. Wesley, 'The Church's One Foundation')

Now concerning the times and the seasons . . . you do not need to have anything written to you. For you yourselves know very well that the day of the Lord will come like a thief in the night.

(1 Thessalonians 5:1)

The last gasp of time
Is thy first breath.

(Henry Vaughan, 'The Evening Watch')

Ancient Christian apocalyptic thinking had its roots in the failure of the Prophetic view of time. Indeed, at all times in history, the apocalyptic consciousness appears to flourish when there is a crisis of faith in human progress. Western culture has been experiencing just such a crisis over the past century. The human tragedies of the twentieth century and the failure of so many of our 'civilising' projects mean that our confidence in progress is frail and damaged. In these conditions the Apocalyptic view of time has a particular appeal. If we believe that we can no longer organise the future, there is little choice but to wait for what will come.

The Prophetic view of time depends upon a massive act of faith, and when this faith is lost the prophetic confidence in the future evaporates. Prophetic time can only operate where people still *believe* in the human capacity for self-improvement. The process of self-improvement may be seen as something divinely planned, or as a purely human venture. But when the underlying belief in improvement goes, when we simply have no more confidence in human history, then we will find the Prophetic mode of time giving way to time in the Apocalyptic mode. Work will give way to waiting, planning will give way to watching, confidence will give way to hope. Just such a shift took place when the ancient Jewish culture lost confidence in its prophets and turned instead to apocalyptic and messianic visionaries.

If we look back at the biblical prophets we see powerful communicators with instructive ethical-political messages to deliver. The prophets speak in the context of a two-way relationship between God and his people. Human history evolves as God and Israel interact. Through the prophets, God urges the people to act righteously or suffer the consequences. Amos warns against social injustice and empty religiosity; Isaiah warns against idolatry; Habakkuk predicts 'trouble' for those engaged in economic exploitation. The prophets are *corrective*, because they still believe – however faintly – that human history can be mended, that human endeavours are still worth the biscuit. For the prophets there is still some *point* in delivering the message of God, in giving second chances and new beginnings.

But for the writers of the apocalyptic tradition, the human experiment has simply failed. The time for threats and warnings is over. Humanity has had its hour in the Last Chance Saloon. God must now step in to wind up the sorry story of human history and impose a new world order.

The book of Daniel gives us a good flavour of the full-blown apocalyptic consciousness. Daniel tells us that ordinary human history – which he calls the era of the four kingdoms – will be replaced by a new kingdom of God. The earthly kingdoms will be smashed by 'a stone cut by no human hand' – in other words the closure of human history will not be part of an historical logic or progression, but an extra-historical intervention by God. Unlike the prophets, Daniel has no faith in humans as agents of historical change: everything is now in God's hands:

> Blessed be the name of God for ever and ever,
> To whom belong wisdom and might.
> He changes times and seasons;
> He removes kings and sets up kings.   (Daniel 2:20–21)

Daniel's visions are mythical rather than historical: strange beasts, cosmic armies, and mysterious apparitions. Human history is now essentially redundant, the only thing that matters is the age to come, and the only thing one can do is to be ready when the hour falls. Daniel warns people to use the time before the apocalypse to prepare themselves by putting an end to sin and dedicating themselves to holiness. But these preparations will not change the outcome. The time of the future apocalypse has been sealed. Israel's doom has already been assigned and when it comes it will be devastating.

In a chilling passage in chapter 10, Daniel foretells the pointless, treacherous and savage story of future human history. This history will be sheer tragedy, an era of sword and flame, betrayal and blasphemy. Eventually the wrath of God will reach bursting point. This will be 'a time of great distress, unparalleled since nations first came into existence'. The wise and holy know they can do nothing to avert the doom to come, and must simply hold out for the Time of the End, when they will be spared.

The pre-Christian apocalyptic consciousness is also closely tied up with messianic expectation. Daniel speaks about 'one like a son of Man' who will oversee the kingdom of God, echoing the messianic message of Isaiah. The messiah is a kind of liquidator – a wonderful counsellor, mighty judge – sent in to wind up the affairs of human history. The messiah ensures that justice will be at the heart of the apocalypse. The events to come may be terrible, many may suffer and die, there may be untold destruction – but the messiah will save the righteous and lead them into the new kingdom. The righteous just need to keep their nerve and stand firm as the corrupt structures of human history collapse around them.

Jesus arrives in the biblical narrative as an unashamedly apocalyptic figure with an uncompromising apocalyptic message. The kingdom of God – its character, structure, values and timing – are the centrepiece of Jesus' preaching. There are many explicitly apocalyptic passages in Jesus' teaching, notably his description in Mark 13 about a 'time of tribulation' before the coming of the Son of Man. This passage is thoroughly developed and expanded by both Matthew (chapter 24) and Luke (chapters 17 and 21). All conclude with the injunction to be ready and alert for the re-appearance of the messiah. Mark sums up the essence of Apocalyptic time most succinctly: 'What I say to you, I say to all: Watch!' (13:37)

An A type ethic of readiness was central to the identity of the earliest Christians who believed that Jesus would come again in their own lifetime. The prospect of the imminent end of history concentrated the mind of the early Church wonderfully. Making plans for the future was pointless – even plans for marriage. Challenging political authorities was futile – these, St Paul said, had all been appointed by God. There simply was no future for human projects. 'The night is far gone, the day is at hand' (Romans 13:12). The only time that mattered was the era of the forthcoming kingdom. So *this* time – the remaining passage of human time – must be spent in 'eager longing' and preparation. Paul expressed the apocalyptic faith in an eloquent passage from his letter to the Romans (8:18–23):

I consider that the sufferings of this present time
are not worth comparing with the glory that is to be
    revealed to us.
For the creation waits with eager longing
for the revealing of the sons of God;
for the creation was subjected to futility,
    not of its own will
but by the will of him who subjected it in hope;
that the creation itself will be set free
    from its bondage to decay
and obtain the freedom
    of the glory of the children of God.
We know that the whole creation
has been groaning in travail together until now;
and not only the creation, but we ourselves,
who have the first fruits of the Spirit,
groan inwardly as we wait for adoption as sons,
the redemption of our bodies.

Paul buttressed the apocalyptic faith of the early Church with a powerful theology of sin and human powerlessness. The problem with all human projects is human sin. Even the best-intentioned plans will go wrong. 'I can will what is right' argued Paul, 'but I cannot do it. For I do not do the good I want, but the evil I do not want is what I do.' (Romans 7:18–19) So the promise of the future 'rests on grace' not human endeavour (Romans 4:16). The future kingdom cannot be a human work, but can only be God's gift. We cannot force this gift or determine it in any way. We can only *hope* for it.

As it turned out, the much longed-for messiah did not come, which forced a crisis in the Christian view of time. The delay or failure of the apocalypse was not the end of apocalyptic faith. But this faith would now have to revise its thinking of the apocalypse. (We see this revision even in the course of the New Testament. See the discussion of the Letter to the Ephesians in Chapter Six.) The ever-present possibility of death still presented the individual with a personal apocalyptic horizon. And, as we shall see in the rest of this chapter, an A type faith could still be constructed upon an apocalyptic view of spiritual waiting. Ironically, the belief in an imminent cosmic apocalypse – so much the bread and butter of the first Church – has increasingly became a secular obsession: a concern with the technological and social risks of human progress.

An anatomy of waiting

Waiting is life.

(Victor Hugo, *L'Autographe*)

They also serve who only stand and wait.

(John Milton, 'On His Blindness')

What is real
About us all is that each is of us is waiting.

(W. H. Auden, *For the Time Being*)

The essence of Apocalyptic time is waiting. Those in A type time are all waiting, although they may all be waiting for very different things, and waiting in very different ways. Whether the apocalypse is cataclysmic, benevolent or even infinitely deferred is not the primary issue. St Paul and Samuel Beckett both saw time as Apocalyptic, even though their views of 'apocalypse' were worlds apart. To get under the skin of Apocalyptic time we need to explore the character of waiting, the different kinds of waiting and their uses.

Waiting is commonly regarded as wasted time. We are encouraged in our working lives to be useful, to 'make a difference', to be productive, to make every minute count *towards* something. Being 'busy' is taken to be an automatic good. We admire activists, shakers and movers, those who 'seize the day', 'use time well' and 'get things done'. At best we take waiting to be a necessary evil. For this reason we do not often think about our times of waiting. We do not stop to *feel* what it is like to wait. We just try to get waiting over with as quickly as possible. However, if we do stop to feel the quality of our times of waiting we will become aware that waiting is not a simple state, but a complex range of states, each with a quite different character and religious significance.

Apocalyptic waiting is not just an attitude towards a final apocalypse, but a way of approaching the appearance of truth at every point in life. Instead of *planning* the future, we *remain open* to it, receptive to what each day may bring, receptive to each person we meet. The person who waits attentively is also one who watches and listens. So waiting is not passive, but an *active openness* to possibility. Once taken as a religious attitude, waiting is not the blank space between events, but a way of approaching all human existence. The person in A type time is radically attentive to life as a process of on-going revelation. So waiting is not emptiness, but attentive concern, as W. H. Vanstone has argued in *The Stature of Waiting*. Waiting implies a positive interest in the future and its outcome. Whether we wait in trepidation, uncertainty or expectation, our waiting means that we *care* about what may come. This concern may indeed take the form of intense activity, if waiting time is used in preparation for the coming future.

So the opposite of waiting is not activity but *boredom*, a state of indifference to the outcome of time. The bored person has lost interest in the future and is no longer waiting, but marking time. The bored person has not only forgotten what time is for, but no longer cares what time is for. Caring nothing for the outcome of time, the bored person has succumbed to moral and religious laziness. Waiting, by contrast, calls for specific virtues: endurance, hope, faithfulness and patience.

Once we start to reflect upon waiting we see that it has four distinct modes: 'expectation', 'awaiting', 'apprehension' and 'open waiting'. Much of our day-to-day waiting takes the form of *expectation*. We are expecting something particular to arrive at a particular time – a phone call, a special event, the delivery of a parcel. We know what we are waiting for and we know how long we will have to wait for it. Expectation is the most closed form of waiting with the least risk and the least degree of uncertainty. Unless we are waiting eagerly for something very special – say a birthday – we tend not to notice this kind of waiting. We do this waiting alongside other activities. But it's always there; we are always waiting expectantly for lists of scheduled events to happen.

As it becomes more uncertain, more *risky*, waiting becomes more interesting. The more uncertain our waiting becomes, the more powerless we are, the more beholden we become to what each day will bring. When we know *what* we are waiting for, but *we do not know when* it will arrive, waiting takes the form of *awaiting*. Isaiah, John the Baptist and Simeon are all *awaiters*. They all anticipate the coming of a messiah, but the timing of his birth is not known. The return of Jesus is also awaited. Jesus tells his disciples that he will come again, but only the Father knows the hour. Even the Son and all the angels will have to await the apocalypse (Matthew 24:36). As a result many will be caught out. Those who await must be constantly vigilant, like sentries. For St Paul, the entire Church is in a state of awaiting, 'groaning inwardly' as he puts it, for the *parousia*.

The uncertainty of waiting deepens when the object of waiting is not known and can only be looked forward to with *apprehension*. In everyday life we might experience apprehension when waiting for exam results, or a medical diagnosis. We know *when* the news will come, but we do not know *what* it will be. Our future health, safety and happiness are bundled up with events we cannot control or predict, we can only wait for them in apprehension.

The most uncertain, and the most interesting form of waiting is *open waiting*, when we remain open to what the future will bring without pre-judgement or expectation. In open waiting we cannot be sure what we are waiting for or how long it will take. So we are open to the truth with a completely receptive attitude. We have not decided in advance what the truth will be, or even what God will be. The point is to let God be God. Open waiting shows the true essence of waiting, waiting in its purest form. In one of his sermons Paul Tillich describes open waiting as

> Waiting in inner stillness, with poised tension and open-
> ness toward what we can only receive. Such openness
> is highest activity; it is the driving force which leads us
> towards the growth of something new in us.

The positive religious potential of open waiting is worth some further exploration. In one of the sections that follow I will focus this exploration on two distinctive early twentieth-century thinkers: Simone Weil and Walter Benjamin. Both thinkers, in different but complementary ways, develop the idea of Apocalyptic waiting as an antidote to a modern culture fixated with progress, systems and production.

Post-modern apocalypse 1: the chips of messianic time

A present apocalypse could only be an apocalypse of
our actual emptiness.

(Thomas Altizer, *Genesis and Apocalypse*)

To detach ourselves from all good things and to wait.
Experience proves that this waiting is satisfied.
It is then we touch the absolute good.

(Simone Weil, *Gravity and Grace*)

Attentiveness is the natural prayer of the soul.

(Nicolas Malebranche)

Every second is the straight gate
through which the Messiah might enter.

(Walter Benjamin, 'Theses on the Philosophy of
History')

So far as we know Walter Benjamin and Simone Weil were not
acquainted. They could have met, possibly in the late 1920s when
Weil was studying at the Ecole Normale Supérieure in Paris. Who
knows? But together they make a fascinating pair: parallel lives
lived in the first half of the twentieth century, parallel lines of
thought about time.

Weil and Benjamin both came from Jewish families. Weil became
an unusual kind of Christian (she refused to be baptised) and
Benjamin remained an unusual kind of Jew. Both were outsiders,
and never quite part of any movement. Benjamin dabbled at the
edges of the famous Frankfurt School but Weil was simply too
freakish to be part of anything. Benjamin was wealthy enough not
to worry about work. Weil – despite various efforts to identify with
the workers on the factory floor – found it hard to hold down a
job. Significantly, each committed suicide. On 26 September 1940
Walter Benjamin took his life at the Franco-Spanish border
believing that his bid to escape Nazi Germany had failed and that
he would now be facing a death camp. Simone Weil died in
Ashford, Kent in August 1943 having starved herself to death. Both

had lost faith – in a radical and personal way – in the prospects for future time. In suicide they both brought on the apocalypse.

As philosophers, Weil and Benjamin shared a belief in the fragmentary character of time. Neither had any faith in a systematic view of history, or the value of the Big Picture, or in great plans for historical improvement. The question of time's meaning had to be worked out in the now, in the space of happening that we call 'the present moment'. Both thinkers were very taken with Malebranche's maxim, that 'attentiveness is the natural prayer of the soul' and both saw the engagement with the present as a religious event.

The common reference point for Weil and Benjamin's suspicion of progress was Marxism. Both started out as orthodox Marxists, but both quickly lost faith in Marx's progressive view of history. Marxism depends upon a classic P type view of time – the conviction that history has a goal and that we can work towards it. Marxism is 'a cause' that will change history. In the wake of one world war and in the midst of a second, Weil and Benjamin simply didn't believe in the promises of Marxist theory. Human history seemed to them to be fundamentally 'tragic'.

Benjamin tried to crystallise the tragedy of history in a single image 'the angel of history' given in his 'Theses on the Philosophy of History':

> His eyes are staring, his mouth is open, his wings are spread. This is how one pictures the angel of history. His face is turned toward the past. Where we perceive a chain of events, he sees one single catastrophe, which keeps piling wreckage upon wreckage and hurls it in front of his feet. The angel would like to stay, awaken the dead, and make whole what has been smashed. But a storm is blowing from Paradise; it has got caught in his wings with such violence that the angel can no longer close them. This storm irresistibly propels him into the future to which his back is turned, while the pile of debris before him grows skyward. This storm is what we call progress.

Simone Weil was equally pessimistic: 'Human history is simply the history of the servitude which makes men – oppressors and oppressed alike – the plaything of the instruments of domination they themselves have manufactured, and thus reduces living humanity to being the chattel of inanimate chattels . . . From time to time the oppressed manage to drive out one team of oppressors and to replace it by another . . . it would seem that man is born a slave, and that servitude is his natural condition.' Benjamin puts it more succinctly: 'the continuum of history is that of the oppressor'.

If the lifting of oppression will not come from within history, then it must come by some divine reconfiguration of history, by an apocalyptic event that blasts its way into the historical order. This event cannot be demanded or forced; it can only be desired and awaited. Benjamin and Weil did not react to the tragedy of history with despair – at least, not until the very end – but with messianic hope.

Benjamin said that we encounter time 'in images, not stories': 'The true picture of the past flits by,' he said. 'The past can be seized only as an image which flashes up at the instant when it can be recognised and is never seen again.' Benjamin called these instants *Jetztzeit* or 'now time'. This was a conception of 'now' in an Apocalyptic rather than a Kairic sense. The 'now' was an opening for impending revelation, not an epiphany of meaning. The whole of history, said Benjamin, 'is shot through with chips of messianic time'. Any moment might be 'the straight gate through which the messiah will enter'. Benjamin was not thinking of a literal messiah, but of the arrival of messianic justice and truth. The longing for justice becomes an apocalyptic task. 'Only the Messiah himself consummates all history, in the sense that he alone redeems, completes, creates its relation to the Messianic. Therefore the Kingdom of God is not a telos . . . it cannot be set as a goal.'

Weil believed that we must adopt an attitude that she called *attente*. *Attente* means 'waiting'. To be *en attente* means to be 'pending' or 'in abeyance' or 'on hold'. This could give the impression of a passive attitude. However, Weil's *attente* was an active attention to a definite object. She saw *attente* as the door to truth, beauty and goodness. *Attente* is also the basic attitude of prayer, indeed of right living in general. In the state of *attente* we are letting God be God without any prejudgement of what God is.

Weil argued that we must 'cease to make the future our objective' and 'wait for God' in the continual arrival of the present. It is an appealing idea – albeit rather bleak and ascetic.

Benjamin and Weil are the patron saints of those politically concerned people who despair of politics, of those who read the daily papers and see only the tragic consequences of human power, of those who have more faith in the apocalyptic transformation of oppression than in human projects of liberation.

Post-modern apocalypse 2: the everyday apocalypse

I still have faith in the sense of wanting to slow down and wait, wait, wait upon Being.

(Don Cupitt, *The Religion of Being*)

Forests spread
Brooks plunge
Rocks persist
Mist diffuses

Meadows wait
Springs well
Winds dwell
Blessing muses

(Martin Heidegger, 'On the Experience of Thinking')

All things counter, original, spare, strange;
Whatever is fickle, freckled (who knows how?)
With swift, low; sweet, sour; adazzle, dim;
He fathers-forth whose beauty is past change: praise
him.

(Gerard Manley Hopkins, 'Pied Beauty')

One of the most remarkable films of the last decade was Paul Thomas Anderson's *Magnolia* (1999). The climax of the film comes when frogs rain down from the skies over the dwellings and inhabitants of Los Angeles. It's a difficult spectacle to take in. The rain of frogs doesn't connect with the rest of the narrative, it just arrives as a random event, as 'just one of those things'. We are left asking, 'what's going on?' and 'what does it mean?'

In fact nothing is 'going on' and the rain of frogs has no meaning. This is just an episode in life – admittedly a remarkable episode – but no more 'meaningful' than the normal kind of rain. Raining frogs is almost unheard of, but not quite. In freak weather conditions it really does happen. On 12 July 1873 frogs fell from the sky in Kansas City. On 3 August 1883 there was a shower of frogs in Cairo, Illinois. In October 1942 the same thing happened again in Buffalo. In June 1997 toads were deposited by a tornado on the Mexican town of Sineloa. Truth, as they say, can be stranger than fiction.

In *Magnolia* Anderson tries to show the sheer contingency of life – the way things just happen without being part of any grand narrative or carrying any special message. The everyday random happenings – chance meetings, accidents and unexpected weather – we take for granted. Anderson uses the raining frogs to open our eyes to a universe of random possibilities. The characters are all waiting and hoping for some kind of love or affirmation in their lives. But the arrival of love cannot be coerced or managed. Love, if it comes at all, arrives as 'just one of those things'. This is a radical apocalyptic vision of life as the occurrence of chance events. Magnolia shows that the apocalypse need not be a future event. The very ongoing happening of the world can be thought of as 'apocalyptic', as a constant revelation of existence.

Try this exercise in Apocalyptic time: take an apple, cut it in half and look at the inside. What you are looking at has never been seen before. You are the first. As you cut the apple there is a second or two of waiting. Then there is the revelation, the sudden appearance of something fresh and entirely new. That apple, in your hands at this time, with all the particularities of time and place – this is all unique. If you think about it, all experience is like this. What you see and sense *right now* is entirely particular and unique to *you*. All experience can be seen as an on-going revelation.

The trouble is that even the experience of utter newness can become banal. If you've sliced one apple, you've sliced them all. We become blind to the astonishing apocalypse of everyday experience. You and I do not know what is just about to happen or what we are just about to see. Just reflect upon your experience at this very moment: your hands holding the book, your eyes scanning the text. You don't know what I'm going to say next. It's a revelation. All this experience is coming at you, fresh as water, like a wave from a hidden sea.

The most powerful contemporary theological advocate of this apocalypse of everyday becoming is Don Cupitt. Time has always been a fundamental issue in Cupitt's writing. We are historical animals who live and die in time. We are 'time' as much as we are 'flesh'. Life is an ongoing *event* that Cupitt has called 'ecstatic immanence'.

In his most recent writing Cupitt has moved closer and closer to a mystical-apocalyptic view of time. His earlier emphasis upon the creative activity of religion in forming meanings and making values has given way to a 'religion of Being'. The point of this religion is not so much to *create* as to *be*. Cupitt urges us to position ourselves within Being, so that the happening of life can present itself to us. The shift has been away from Nietzsche's radical humanism and towards the mysticism of Being that we find in the late writings of Martin Heidegger.

Cupitt's recent writing is full of examples of everyday apocalypse. In *The Revelation of Being* he describes the childhood experience of seeing a girl of the same age: 'I saw her blonde hair against the declining sun, which appeared to set her hair on fire and make her look like a heavenly visitant.' In *The Religion of Being* Cupitt praises the sheer given-ness 'of the most transient beauties: water, spray, rainbows, clouds, flying insects, birds, shadows, flowers, moments of love and friendship'. Such moments of everyday revelation are, for Cupitt, what counts as religious experience. He excludes the possibility of otherworldly revelations seeing the world of ordinary experience as a complete revelation of reality. This is it. What you see is what you get.

Living in time is an ongoing wonder, an ever-unfolding revelation of being, taking place at every minute in a shimmering wave of liquid happening. To feel the exhilarating flux of Being we must try to surf time, balanced on its crest as its surges forth.

Try to sit completely on the leading edge of Now. If you

> can do it it is ravishing... one feels snatched away,
> transported. *And* it costs nothing.

This reference to Now has a kairic feel. But Cupitt doesn't see time as a succession of kairic moments, but as a continuous torrent of experience. It is apocalyptic because as he says, we must 'wait, wait, wait upon Being'. Being is not our project, or even our special moment, it is something we behold – in astonishment. 'Life comes at us' he says 'not necessitated, but contingent and largely unpredictable'.

The connections between Cupitt's apocalypse and the Revelation of St John may seem very slight. What links them is not their view of the apocalypse – these could hardly be more different, but the feeling of Apocalyptic time as a form of waiting. Having said that, Cupitt's metaphors for the revelation of Being have a traditional apocalyptic feel. He describes revelation as 'a slow motion explosion', a fountain, a burning fire and a blazing sun. The distant resonance with traditional apocalyptic motifs is unmistakable – all these images can be found in the Book of Revelation: the collapse of the world's cities, the springs of living water; the lake of fire; the angels with faces shining like the sun. But Cupitt's apocalypse is the very opposite of a cataclysmic 'time of the End': Revelation is happening now. *This* is it, your *life* is it, even as you read these words.

Post-modern apocalypse 3: imagination and risk

> What no eye has seen
> Nor ear heard
> Nor the heart of man conceived.
>
> (1 Corinthians 2:9)

> Behold, a great image. This image mighty, and of exceeding brightness, stood before you, and its appearance was frightening.
>
> (Daniel 2:31)

> Apocalypse has become banal, a set of statistical risk parameters to everyone's existence.
>
> (Anthony Giddens, *Modernity and Self Identity*)

80

One of the curious things about the apocalyptic imagination has been its sheer durability. The idea of the apocalypse – of a fantastic future beyond the horizon of prediction and historical calculation – has fired the imagination of writers and artists down the centuries. The Revelation of St John, Shakespeare's *The Tempest* and Milton's *Paradise Lost* all show us fantastic worlds that act as a commentary on this one. But it is in the twentieth century, arguably, that apocalyptic film and literature have developed into a pervasive artistic genre, fuelled by hopes and fears about the potential of science to sculpt the shape of future history.

But the 'future' of the apocalypse is beyond any immediate historical horizon. The apocalyptic writer does not have to show how we get from 'here' to 'there' – apocalyptic worlds are not connected to our time by a chain of plausible historical developments. There is no historical narrative that connects our world with Huxley's *Brave New World*, Orwell's *Nineteen Eighty-Four* or Fritz Lang's *Metropolis*. These are not future histories but self-contained fictions connected to our world by strings of analogy and hyperbole. They are held up in order to effect a new understanding – a new revelation – of the world of human history. Apocalyptic worlds are not realist predictions but parables – they set our world side by side with another for creative comparison. As J. G. Ballard puts it, apocalyptic worlds are 'extreme metaphors'.

The continuing power of the apocalyptic imagination is shown in the huge success of Philip Pullman's *His Dark Materials* trilogy. Pullman is a writer in the classic apocalyptic mode, showing us over three volumes a fantastic cosmic battle between God and his creatures. His universe is peopled by mythic creatures, and agents of light and darkness. The action takes place, as it does in the Book of Revelation, in extreme locations including the very depths of hell itself. Pullman sets this entire cosmic scenario in a series of parallel universes layered alongside our own, but not directly connected with any human historical time. It is ironic that a writer who is so evangelical about his atheism should have chosen such a typically theological mode of narration.

In essence the apocalyptic imagination is an attempt to short-circuit time, to leap across the space of apocalyptic waiting and grasp the vision in advance. Instead of waiting upon revelation, the apocalyptic artist previews the apocalyptic image for us. The apocalyptic artist is fired with an impatient desire to bring the revelation forward, to provide us with a warning or an advertisement about the latent potential of the present. If we had to sum up the apocalyptic message in one phrase it would be Daniel's announcement to King Nebuchadnezzar: 'Behold, a great image!'

Although apocalyptic writers often use plot and characterisation to great effect, apocalyptic literature is primarily a descriptive genre. In apocalyptic visions the world-picture is more important than the story. There is a plot of sorts in the Revelation of St John, but John's real mission is panoramic: to tell us 'what he sees'. Most of sections of the book begin with a phrase like *'kai eidon'* ('and I saw'), giving the impression of someone slowly taking in a vast, complex landscape. Any narration takes place against this commanding backdrop. We see much the same in modern apocalyptic fiction, where the plot is always competing with the writer's lavish description of 'the system'. Orwell's *Nineteen Eighty-Four* is primarily a vision of a political system. The main function of the hero, Winston Smith, is to act as our window onto Orwell's dystopia. Similarly, the point of Margaret Atwood's *The Handmaid's Tale* is to show us the Republic of Gilead. The concluding chapter describes the novel as a 'monotheocracy seen through a diary'. Atwood tells us that the heroine Offred 'was one of many, and must be seen within the broad outlines of the moment of history of which she was a part'. As for Huxley's *Brave New World* – can any of us remember much at all about the characters or the plot? It is for this reason that apocalyptic novels rarely make successful popular cinema: they work as spectacles, but fail as stories. The narration, however powerful, is always dwarfed by the scale and importance of the apocalyptic landscape.

The modern apocalyptic imagination tends to experience time as fearful awaiting. The future takes the form of a danger that must be averted. This may mobilise us into frantic activity that looks liked P type behaviour. But A type activity is quite different. Whereas P type activity works systematically towards an historical goal, A type activity is directed towards risk management and damage limitation. The A type activist is more like a fire fighter, the P type activist like a town planner. The A type activist is concerned with *risks*, the P type activist with *opportunities*.

If the modern apocalyptic imagination keeps presenting us with visions of risk and danger, what is its attraction? Apocalyptic film and literature speaks directly to our contemporary anxiety about risk. One of the defining characteristics of our age is a new form of risk: not the risk posed by the natural world, but the risk posed by cultural 'progress'. The daily newspapers can read like a catalogue of risks – BSE, AIDS, nuclear power, genetically modified crops, globalisation – we are all living under apocalyptic conditions, fearful of a range of known and unknown dangers. Two contemporary sociologists, Ulrich Beck and Anthony Giddens, have argued that we now understand our lives and our future fundamentally in terms of risk. Ulrich Beck has called our world in general a 'risk society'. In Beck's analysis, the social, political and technological progress of the modern period has thrown up innumerable dangers. Social progress has endangered traditional forms of social organisation such as marriage and the family. The development of technology has inflicted global ecological and medical damage. And so on. So we live life apocalyptically in the shadow of a vast number of present and future risks:

> The utopia of the risk society remains *negative* and *defensive*. Basically, one is no longer concerned with attaining something 'good', but rather with *preventing* the worst; self-limitation is the goal which emerges.

For Beck our risk consciousness takes the form of *anxiety*. We not only fear the risks we know, but we wait in apprehension for latent risks, which have yet to emerge. And so we become fearful of the future in general. Since tomorrow may throw up some new hazard, time itself – in other words *just staying alive* – becomes a constant risk. In 1998 the cinema-going public was treated to two Hollywood films about meteors heading towards planet earth: *Deep Impact* and *Armageddon*. A 'risk society' is bound to find special meaning in films about impending cataclysm.

Anthony Giddens has plotted what he sees as a fundamental change in the 'climate of risk'. In a developing industrial society, he says, risks are 'calculated' and are an integral part of progress. In other words risks are actively 'taken' and accepted as part and parcel of the cost of human advancement. These are controlled or as we say 'calculated risks'. But we have entered a new age of risk, Giddens argues, in which the hazards of progress cannot be

83

calculated. No one knows the effects that may be caused by, say, GM crops or global warming. These risks are not part of any plan. Such risks drive us to understand our lives in terms of 'precaution', 'defence', coping', 'protection' and 'containment'. As Giddens puts it, 'apocalypse has become banal, a set of statistical risk parameters to everyone's existence'. We can only prepare ourselves as best we can and await the outcome of the future. Simple survival – rather than progress – will be counted as success. Our modern risk culture bears some comparison with St Paul and the early Church. Whereas the members of the early Church were on their knees praying to be spared in the apocalypse, the members of our modern 'risk society' are buying organic produce and popping vitamin pills.

In the face of a high consciousness of risk, time loses historical purpose. The time of the future is not something we can work towards. As we will see in Chapter Five, one response to risk is to retreat into non-progressive K type time and simply enjoy what beauty and meaning we can find in life's occasional epiphanies. But between these moments time is empty, a space to be filled defensively with pastimes, rituals, games, routines and habits – like Vladimir and Estragon waiting for Godot. In its worst form, the apocalyptic consciousness understands time simply as 'dead time' that needs to be 'killed'. We 'keep ourselves busy', 'pass the time of day' and 'let the hours go by'. But without any real hope, without a 'future' in the positive sense of the word.

One could apply a risk analysis to the historical consciousness of the church. Is the church in Europe now perhaps in an apocalyptic mode, driven by the fear of the risk of its own extinction? Is the goal now simply to *survive* the worst that secularism can throw at it? Undoubtedly this is true of some churches and congregations. Such churches may look busy, active and energetic. But busy for what purpose? Their main task will be to 'preserve' something – perhaps a set of internal relationships, an idea of the true faith', or particular religious practices – but there will be no historical vision beyond survival. These are churches 'holding on' – perhaps under the banner of 'tradition', 'heritage' or 'orthodoxy'. But if you ask them what they would like the church in general or the world to look like in fifty or a hundred or a thousand years time, they will simply want things to 'be the same'. This is because they think of time as something to be endured, as a space to be filled with more of the same. They have no theory or vision of how time will progress or where 'progress' is leading. Indeed they do not believe in progress, full stop. If threats to Christianity continue to multiply with the advance of secularism, there is a risk that the church may slip increasingly into defensive, A type thinking. This would produce – if it hasn't happened already – a survivalist organisation, permanently in attrition against perceived 'threats' and with no vision for its own future.

CHAPTER FIVE

Kairic (or K type) Time

Lost in time

> Time is dealt out by particles, and each
> One mingled with the streaming sands of life.
> > (Edward Young, *Night Thoughts*)

> The mode of Being exists only in the here and now.
> > (Erich Fromm, *To Have or To Be*)

> Magic moments, when two hearts are carin'
> Magic moments, mem'ries we've been sharing.
> > (Perry Como, 'Magic Moments')

It's easy enough to feel lost in time – after all there is so much of it. The lives of entire civilisations barely register as dots on the time-line of the universe. The entire history of humanity, from prehistory to the personal computer, is just a blink of the eye of time. The individual human life is less than a blink – a fraction of a fraction. And an individual action – say the reading of these words – is almost nothing at all. If we think of time on the grand scale, it is hard to give any weight at all to the fleeting passage of our lives. If we want to understand *human time*, the grand scale is perhaps not the best place to start. Better perhaps to start at the other end, with the dots and blinks that make up the scale. There would, after all, be no minutes without seconds, or years without days. The grand scale could be seen as just a sum of moments. And without those moments, would it exist at all?

To view time in this way would be to see time as granular, like sand, made up of episodes or epiphanies that have an internal logic and value of their own, rather than taking their meaning from the great scheme of history as a whole. The point of such a history would be to understand each episode in its own terms, attentive to the possibilities of each moment. In such a history the 'end' of time would be hauled back from the future and re-located in the very middle of life. Each moment – even now, here in this very moment – would be an historical end in itself.

I was prompted to start the journey towards ordination as a priest by a Buddhist monk taking photographs on a beach in South Korea. I asked him about his photography and he explained that he had no film in his camera, but was using it to help him focus upon the visual beauty of each moment. I laughed and he joined in. The conversation only lasted a few minutes, but has stayed with me ever since. That monk alerted me to the religious potential of 'the moment'. The moment is so very simple, so manageable, so available. I felt liberated from anxiety about where things would lead, or what the future would hold. It seemed to me that I merely had to be attentive to the moment and its opportunities. If I took care of the minutes, the years would take care of themselves. Later, after a theological education, I learnt that this idea of the 'moment' had a theological name: *kairos*, an ancient Greek term used by Jesus and St Paul to mean 'the right time'. Before Christ, the term had been used by philosophers to describe rhetorical timing, the 'right moment' for making a remark. In Jesus and Paul, the term became eschatological, a way of speaking about the timing of salvation, in other words the very essence of sacred time.

In this chapter I will be using the terms *kairos* and Kairic time in a wider sense than Jesus intended. What I am calling Kairic, or K type, time refers to any view of history as a series of moments each potentially complete in itself. This includes the biblical *kairos*, but is not restricted to it. We find the K type view powerfully present in Christian mysticism, particularly in the idea of 'the sacrament of the present moment'. Beyond Christianity, the K type view of time is prevalent in a range of secular literature and philosophy. Indeed in our own age, the K type view of time is enjoying tremendous popularity. In this chapter I will examine some of the rich thinking of K time, looking both at the attraction of this view and its dangers.

The pre-Christian *kairos*: opportunity and decorum

In an oration, as in life, nothing is harder to determine than what is appropriate.

(Cicero)

And who are you?
– Kairos, who subdues all things.
And why do you stand on tip-toe?
– I am ever running.

(Epigram on the statue of Kairos by Lysippos)

In ancient thought *kairos* was not just an idea, but a mythical figure: a young man, usually naked with winged feet and long hair hanging over his face. In some cases he is shown fleeing from a crowd who are seeking to grasp him by the forelock. In his hands he may be carrying a pair of scales to show that his time is the time of judgement. For extra effect the scales may be balanced on a knife-edge. Usually those reaching for him are not nearly swift enough and he flies away, leaving them to rue their lost opportunity. There was, allegedly, a statue to the god Kairos outside the stadium at Olympia – perhaps a message to athletes to seize their moment. The ancient *kairoi* were windows for human action within the fateful passage of chronological time. The *kairos* was a unique moment of decision, responsibility and destiny.

The philosophy of *kairos* also had a place in the ancient theory of rhetoric. The kairic orator measures his speech to the occasion, discerning the nuances of a situation and choosing with care the words which will strike the right note. The orator must be aware of his/her audience and their situation, rather than sounding off with pre-packaged speeches. The desired effect is 'decorum': the right word for the right occasion. Isocrates – a Greek philosopher of the fourth century BC – developed the rhetorical theory of *kairos* into a more general theory of life. He believed that we should try to be decorous not only in speech, but in everything we do. Since life is infinitely varied and no set of circumstances is precisely like any other, our actions must be tailored to the situation. Isocrates called this approach *phronesis* or 'practical insight'. When we practise *phronesis*, we try to deploy our words and actions to best effect.

Isocrates argued, for instance, that we should not get angry when we *feel* angry, but express our anger strategically 'when the occasion demands it'. If we seek, in this manner, to discern the *kairoi* in all areas of life, this will lead us to success and happiness.

The Christian *kairos*: the lilies of the fields

> He has made everything beautiful in its time.
>
> (Ecclesiastes 3:11)

> You know how to interpret the appearance of earth and sky.
> But why do you not know how to interpret the present time [*kairos*]?
>
> (Luke 12:56)

> Consider the lilies of the field
> How they grow;
> They neither toil nor spin.
>
> (Matthew 6:28)

> Every particle of sand in the glass of time is precious to me.
>
> (Augustine, *Confessions*)

In the Bible the *kairos* exists in tension with the view of time as *chronos*. *Chronos* is clock time, the succession of events from past to future. Although the gospel writers use this term as part of their narration, we never hear it used by Jesus. When Jesus talks about time he emphatically uses the word *kairos*. *Kairos* is the very opposite of *chronos*, not time in general, but particular moments of time – the 'hours', 'days', 'seasons' of history. The point here is not the direction of time or its chronological end (*telos*). *Kairos* is the epiphany of time, time distilled into moments or intersections. *Kairos* is a transcendence of *chronos*: *chronos* shows us the series, while *kairos* shows us the episodes. One of the most striking expositions of K type time is Jesus' description of the lilies of the field in the Sermon on the Mount. The point of K type time is to satisfy the ethical and aesthetic potential of every moment. Not only is the future unimportant until it arrives, but a focus on the future may undermine K type existence by dislocating it from the present. Unlike the other three models of time, only K type time is non-linear.

Jesus' thinking of time as *kairos* echoes the teaching about time in the Old Testament wisdom literature, especially Ecclesiastes. The famous passage from Ecclesiastes 3 offers a view of time as a series of openings or opportunities.

> For everything there is a season
> and a time for every matter under heaven:
> a time to be born, and a time to die;
> a time to plant, and a time to pluck up what is planted;
> a time to kill, and a time to heal;
> a time to break down, and a time to build up;
> a time to weep, and a time to laugh;
> a time to mourn, and a time to dance.
> . . .
> He has made everything beautiful in its time.

The wisdom of time is knowing what each moment is for, discerning at any given time the nature of the opportunity that lies before us.

In St Paul's writings the concept of *kairos* is linked with the New Testament concept of 'now' (*nyn*) as when Paul speaks of the 'now-*kairos*' (Romans 11:5). This is weakly translated as 'the present time' (*RSV*) or 'our own time' (*NJB*). But neither do justice to the power of this Pauline phrase. For Paul the 'now' is the now between the two comings, a moment charged with eschatological expectation. 'The whole of creation has been groaning in travail together until now', writes Paul (Romans 8:22), 'and . . . we groan inwardly as we await for adoption as sons.' The now between the two comings is a moment to be seized. By linking this 'now' with *kairos* Paul produces a super-intensified concept of the present. The present contains everything: the momentum of the salvation history of the past, the anticipation of the completion of that history in the future (a future which may come at any moment), and a living-present window of opportunity for Christian existence. The now-*kairos* is simultaneously (as literary critics call it) 'analeptic' and 'proleptic', both a recollection of the past and an anticipation of the future.

The kairic view of time takes us to the heart of a theology of incarnation. The incarnation was a datable moment in history, a kairic instant. Theologians have spoken about the incarnation as the Christ-Event or the Redemptive-Event. In other words, the very idea of Christ is tied up with an idea of time. There are weak and strong versions of kairic theology. In the weak version (offered for instance by Oscar Cullmann in *Christ and Time*) the *kairos* of the incarnation is a middle point in the time-line of redemption. Redemption is still stretched out on a line from alpha to omega between an origin (*arche*) and an end (*telos*). This *kairos* does not challenge the linear aspect of redemptive time, but gives it shape and structure. By contrast, the strong version of kairic theology sees the incarnation as a fundamental disturbance in the linear model of redemption. The *kairos* of the incarnation brings the *telos* of history into the middle of time. Thereafter every moment becomes a kairic opportunity for communion. The strong *kairos* sees redemption not as a line, but as a dispersal pattern of moments through time, a constellation of openings and epiphanies in the dreary and often tragic chronicle of linear history. The *eschaton* becomes an ever-present possibility, rather than a future hope. Catherine Pickstock's liturgical theology of the real presence of the Eucharist (in *After Writing*) is an example of strong K type thinking. For her, every celebration of the Eucharist is of equal kairic status, Christ is fully present at all of them and the Last Supper has no particular priority.

Jesus' teaching lends itself to both strong and weak versions of kairic theology. He speaks about the kingdom both as a present reality and as a future possibility. Traditionally theologians have felt it necessary either to choose between the different versions or to integrate the two into a more general theology of time. This book takes a different approach. There is a real and irreconcilable tension in Jesus' teaching between the linear (Apocalyptic and Prophetic) and non-linear (Kairic) understandings of time. There is no need to resolve this tension – once we are freed from an either/or logic in theology and a fear of dissonance and non-coherence.

It is not hard to see how the kairic idea of time became the basis

91

for spiritual and liturgical practice. Liturgy takes place for its own sake, in its own time, and not as part of a progression towards the future. The liturgical calendar is an attempt to formalise Kairic time into a programme of seasons and days. The liturgical calendar overlays the chronological calendar with a pattern of kairic moments, each with its own distinctive character. Although there is a linear logic to the calendar – following the story of salvation history – the essence of liturgy is repetitive rather than progressive.

The liturgical *kairos* provides a space for a theological encounter without a concern for the general passage of history. In the mysticism of the moment we do not have to evaluate the consequences of our actions. Our only responsibility is to the moment itself. Everything else is a distraction. The *epiclesis* in eucharistic liturgy (the invocation of the Holy Spirit upon the bread and wine) sums up the essence of the eucharistic *kairos*. In the Eucharist Christ is taken to be 'present' – albeit in different ways according to one's eucharistic theology. Christ is uniquely 'available' or 'accessible' in the Eucharist – so much so that we can 'ingest' him in the form of the eucharistic elements. The Eucharist opens a kairic space for Christ's availability, as John Zizioulas puts it in *Being as Communion*, 'the eucharist . . . is the uniquely privileged moment of the Church's existence'.

Kairic theology is also a notable feature of the mystical and spiritual traditions of the church. The author of *The Cloud of Unknowing* tells us to

> be attentive to time and how you spend it. Nothing is more precious. This is evident when you recall that in one tiny moment heaven may be gained or lost. God, the master of time, never gives the future. He gives only the present, moment by moment.

The most prominent example of kairic spirituality is arguably Jean-Pierre de Caussade's *Self-abandonment to Divine Providence* with its doctrine of 'the sacrament of the present moment'. De Caussade was an eighteenth-century Jesuit who took the view that 'what God ordains for each moment is what is most holy, best and most divine for us. All we need to know is how to recognise his will in the present moment.' This 'obedience to the present moment' releases us from the impossible task of trying to organise the future.

Indeed our duty to the present must be so total, argued de Caussade, that we should not 'consider consequences, causes or reasons'. This is an ultimate deontological ethic, in which duty transcends all pragmatic considerations. It is also, like so much kairic thinking, radically individualistic: '[Holy] souls [are] by their nature solitary, free and detached from everything in order that they may contentedly love God who possesses them in peace and quiet.'

It should come as no surprise to us that the K type mystical view has a strong appeal to poets – Christian and otherwise. T. S. Eliot's *Four Quartets* affirm the vision of history as 'a pattern of timeless moments'. Eliot offers us an understanding of time beyond the mere succession of events (life that 'follows like a tedious argument'). He urges us to seek 'a lifetime burning in every moment'. R. S. Thomas is also fascinated by the power of now. For him 'the moment is history's navel and round it the worlds spin'. The religious quest is to find 'love's moment in a world in servitude to time'. In both Eliot and Thomas, the mysticism of the present or time's fragments, provides an alternative to dogmatic and systematic Christianity. The point is not to get our heads around the big picture, but to find divinity (as Thomas puts it) in 'the interstices where mystery could linger'.

The religious concern with time also extends into allegedly 'secular' poetry. The poet Carol Ann Duffy has written a volume ambiguously titled *Mean Time* in which she affirms the redemptive power of 'moments of grace' – a kiss, the smell of oranges, the sound of the sea – against the 'mean' passage of history. Glyn Maxwell's extraordinary verse novel *Time's Fool* imagines Edmund, a train passenger, destined (like the Flying Dutchman) to travel the railways for eternity. Once every seven years, on Christmas Eve, the train pulls up in Edmund's home town, where he hopes to find redemptive love. The story hinges around these kairic opportunities that open up for Edmund. Edmund's salvation, in the end, depends upon the discovery of the most unexpected opportunity.

In contemporary Christianity, the kairic understanding of time is both powerful and popular. In the face of a fear about the future of Christendom, the church has found refuge in K type theology. The K type church places emphasis upon the existential quality of human being, upon liturgy and upon a mystical theology of the present moment. A K type church will tend to value art, prayer and listening over activism and social criticism. This kairic turn is not unique to Christianity, but is all part and parcel of a deep-seated cultural adoption of Kairic time. It is to the origins and development of this 'post-modern *kairos*' that we now turn.

The post-modern *kairos*

> I craved to seize the whole essence, in the confines of one single photograph.
>> (Henri Cartier-Bresson, *The Decisive Moment*)

> Our age prefers the image to the thing.
>> (Ludwig Feuerbach, *The Essence of Christianity*)

> Our oppressive sense of the transience of everything is more acute since cameras gave us the means to 'fix' the fleeting moment.
>> (Susan Sontag, *On Photography*)

The kairic view of time is the popular wisdom of the present age. We are sceptical about 'progress', we doubt whether salvation can be found in 'work' or 'achievement'. We now seek meaning in 'quality time', in the beauty and happiness of every moment. New Age mysticisms and philosophies emphasise the importance of 'now'. Eckhart Tolle, for example, has recently written about 'the power of now'. Tolle says that we must 'end the delusion of time' and find freedom in the fleeting moment of the present. Tolle's message, although packaged as provocative and transformative, is really a confirmation of something we want to hear: that the world 'out there' is not our problem. The past is not our responsibility and the future is not real at all. There is only Now as we experience it. Instead of striving for future goals we should immerse ourselves in present time. Part of us wants to be released from anxiety about the future and available to enjoy the life of the present moment. The 'now' is 'powerful' not because it is challenging, but because it is reassuring. Kairic time is comfort time, time organised around you-and-only-you. As Eckhart Tolle says, the beauty, truth and joy of time are within you.

The development of the post-modern *kairos* has been fuelled by technologies of recording and reproduction. We can now 'capture the moment' as never before in a photographic image, or on video, or on recording tape. Through the media and the Internet we are connected with the global moment, the ongoing *kairos* of world events. The moments of our lives are now simply more available to us. We can document our personal *kairoi*, store them, edit them, retrieve them, publish and distribute them in ways that were simply unthinkable even a century ago. The French photographer Henri Cartier-Bresson turned the idea of a 'snap-shot' into a theory of what he called 'the decisive moment'. From the flux of possible visual images, the photographer must seize the images that define the overall event. As Cartier-Bresson put it, the decisive image is 'the simultaneous recognition, in a fraction of a second, of the significance of an event as well as the precise organisation of forms which gives that event its proper expression'. Our culture is now wallpapered with 'decisive images' – photographic or otherwise – that seek to define a brand, or a product, or a mood, or an organisation. The mass production of images has changed the way we think. We now think in 'snap-shots'. It is not simply that we *produce* images, we now *expect* the world to appear as a surface of images, and sure enough it does.

Just consider the clothes we wear. These are not just functional 'objects', but formatted images that say who we are. When we get dressed we put on a definitive image. When others see us, they see this image before they see 'us'. And the same goes for our cars, houses, gardens, and the entire range of our consumer choices. Everywhere we go we are projecting ourselves in kairic images that say: 'This is a decisive image of me.'

The prophet who saw most clearly the arrival of the post-modern *kairos* was Friedrich Nietzsche. In August 1881 Nietzsche was walking through woods beside the lake of Silvaplana. He stopped by a large pyramid-shaped stone. At this moment an idea came to him, which he believed to be the most brilliant and important philosophical theory of modern times. He jotted it down on a scrap of paper and scribbled a title: '6000 feet beyond humanity and time.' Nietzsche would call this theory 'the doctrine of the eternal return of the same' and we find it set it out in passages in *The Gay Science, Thus Spoke Zarathustra* and posthumously in *The Will to Power.*

The 'doctrine of eternal return' is a simple enough idea: human history travels in circles, like a carousel. History is, as Nietzsche put it, the eternal 'unconditioned and infinitely re-iterated circulation of all things'. Every event that happens is the repetition of an earlier event. So the events of tomorrow, or next year, or the next millennium will not constitute progress to something new, but the return of something old. If we could look at the whole of history at a glance, beyond humanity and time, we would see not a pattern of development and progression but a sequence of return and repetition. There would be no big story, no logic, no sense to it all – just moments and episodes of this or that kind swirling around and back upon themselves. The end of history, as T. S. Eliot put it, will be to arrive at where we started, again and again. Each moment will not be a step forward, but a repeat of some earlier moment. Every square on the board of life will be 'square one'.

Nietzsche was pleased with this 'triumphant idea' because it represented a truly radical alternative both to Christian history, which he saw as a linear path from sin to salvation, and to the Enlightenment belief in human progress. Christian history, argued Nietzsche, was 'an imaginary teleology', in other words a superstitious belief in a positive end to history. The Enlightenment belief in progress was little more than a secularised version of this, having 'invented the concept "goal"', only with humanity rather than God as the prime agent in bringing about 'salvation' on earth. With their fixation on the future, neither of these philosophies of history could be the basis of a proper affirmation of life in the here-and-now.

Nietzsche believed that the world was not ready to hear this wisdom of the here-and-now. Nineteenth-century Enlightenment culture was, Nietzsche believed, too pleased with, too attached to, its own success and progress. Nietzsche argued that the Western world was dominated by the so-called 'last people', who needed their lives to have a rational purpose. The 'last people' see themselves on the crest of the wave of human progress. For them time must have an arrow. Without this arrow, everything would be aimless and human lives would be a pointless trudge of repetition.

Fifteen hundred years earlier, St Augustine had warned Western culture in *The City of God* about the crucial importance of linear history. If time has no arrow, then how can there be redemption? A circular history, like Nietzsche's, cannot take us anywhere. We would be trapped in square one, never able to walk the line towards salvation. Nietzsche recognised the difficulty of accepting the idea of eternal return, calling it 'the greatest weight', a 'Spirit of Gravity', dragging us downward, like lead, 'lead drops in the ear . . . lead thoughts in the brain', the most bitter kind of tragedy.

But tragedy is tragic only for those who expect something else. Nietzsche saw tragedy as his 'tonic', something to stiffen the human fibre. Only people who had overcome the expectation of improvement, so-called 'over-people' would be able to accept with joy the 'eternal return of the same'. These people will have learned to accept the given-ness of each moment as an event in itself. This will be truly joyful, a proper way of saying 'yes' to life.

In fact Nietzsche believed eternal return to be the highest kind of life-affirmation, because it affirms each moment in its own right and not merely as a stepping stone to the future. Those who believe in historical progress are the true nihilists, he argued, because it is they who declare the future to be everything and the present a mere means to that end. But the sacrifice of today on the altar of tomorrow can never reach a conclusion, because tomorrow never comes. In Nietzsche's mind there could be no more virulent form of nihilism than to deny the intrinsic value of the present moment.

At first glance the doctrine of eternal return looks like a complete repudiation of every kind of Christian view of history. Certainly, eternal return sets itself up as the opposite of traditional 'salvation history'. But the progressive linear model of time is not the only type of history we find in Christianity. Indeed Nietzsche's theory of history as a sequence of moments resembles in many ways the kairic view that Jesus sets out in his teaching about the kingdom. Nietzsche argued that the linear model had suppressed all others, obscuring a richer Christian heritage of thinking about history and time.

Despite his loathing of Christendom, Nietzsche had considerable respect for Jesus himself, as his later writings show. Nietzsche saw Jesus as an exemplary teacher, a 'holy anarchist', whose aim was to 'demonstrate how one ought to live'. But as the church formed under St Paul, Nietzsche believed that Jesus' vision was cynically turned into a religion of life-denial and a contemptible ethic of pity. 'The church is precisely that against which Jesus preached,' wrote Nietzsche in *The Will to Power*, 'the church is the barbarization of Christianity'. Although it may surprise us, Nietzsche not only admired Jesus, but believed that a true Christianity was still 'possible but without the absurd dogmas'. True Christianity will 'not be a belief but a doing, above all a *not*-doing of many things, a different *being*'.

A cardinal error, in Nietzsche's view, was the way the church had put 'the salvation legend in place of the symbolic now-and-always, here and everywhere'. In other words, the Church had repressed Jesus' own non-linear, kairic theology of time. In Nietzsche's estimation, Jesus did preach that history would be fulfilled in the kingdom of God, but he did not place the kingdom within a progressive model of time: 'The kingdom of God does not "come" chronologically-historically, on a certain day in the calendar, something that might be here one day but not the day before: it is an "inward change in the individual," something that comes at every moment and at every moment has not yet arrived.' This 'Jesus of the kingdom' was turned by the church into 'the Redeemer' who promised future beatitude, shifting 'the centre of gravity of life *out* of life into the "Beyond"' thereby depriving 'life as such of its centre of gravity'.

The doctrine of eternal return was a philosophical attempt to bring the centre of gravity back into the midst of life as we live it minute by minute. Blessedness around the corner was not nearly enough for Nietzsche who yearned for the ever-present beatitude of every living moment. We must be able to say 'yes and Amen' to life, even in the face of suffering and uncertainty. Despite all his anti-religious and anti-theological rhetoric, Nietzsche could see that eternal return emanated from a religious source: 'we godless anti-metaphysicians still take our fire, too, from the flame lit by a faith that is thousands of years old . . . Christian faith.'

What Nietzsche saw '6000 feet beyond humanity and time' was perhaps not so much a doctrine that would contradict Christianity as one that could also assist in the recovery of an original Christian vision. Nietzsche thought of himself as the 'antichrist', the prophet of the 'death of God'. But this can give a false impression. More truthfully, Nietzsche was an idoloclast, smashing Christendom's idol of historical progress. In doing so, Nietzsche opens a window upon Christ's own teaching about time as *Kairos*: the view of time as a non-progressive sequence of opportunities for ethical and aesthetic being.

We are the children of Nietzsche's prophecy. As we look back over the history of the past century – a century of genocide, ravenous capitalism, grotesque inequalities, world-destroying technologies and competing fundamentalisms – few of us can be unaware of the failures and shortcomings of the 'Enlightenment Project', indeed of 'projects' in general. In these conditions much of our religious and 'spiritual' culture is in retreat from progress and seeking shelter in a mysticism of the present moment and issues of personal development. Like Nietzsche, we have lost faith in the future as a project that demands our energy and imagination. Our new faith is in a theology of 'now'. Around us we see New Age religions offering individual piety and instant gratification; a society driven by consumption; a quest for immediacy in communication; a suspicion of 'ideology'; short-termism in public policy; voter apathy; and Christian churches ever more absorbed in questions of internal organisation, personal conversion and individual moral conduct. The modernist belief that we really could make the world better is weakening. The present is our new temporal horizon, our safe harbour in the ocean of time.

We can see the post-modern thinking of *kairos* laid out with great clarity and eloquence in one of the most celebrated films of recent times: *American Beauty* (1999, dir: Sam Mendes). *American Beauty* is an evocative and powerful cinematic sermon about the post-modern *kairos*. Its message is that beatitude does not lie in achievements or work, but in an engagement with life's transient moments. The film is the story of the awakening of Lester Burnham, played by Kevin Spacey. Lester is in mid-life crisis, alienated from his wife, his daughter and his work. Indeed Lester is alienated from his own immediate experiences – he 'feels sedated' as if 'in a coma for twenty years'. He 'used to be happy' but has 'lost something' that he now decides to recover. He packs in his job, starts smoking dope, buys himself a bright red 1970 Pontiac Firebird, and does weights in his garage. Lester's adolescent regression, although laughable in itself, liberates him to see a 'higher' kairic philosophy of time. Ironically the full vision of this philosophy only comes to Lester in the seconds before his death.

Lester Burnham also functions as a chorus, speaking to us from beyond the grave – like Lazarus. In a voice-over prologue and epilogue Burnham spells out the moral of the film. Lester tells us that he has learned to feel 'gratitude for every single moment of [his] stupid life'. He tells us that we will all come to realise – sooner or later – that life is made of precious moments of beauty. These kairic moments transcend ordinary clock or narrative time, since each one constitutes 'an ocean of time'. It is in these moments that we find our salvation.

By contrast Lester's wife Carolyn is one of Nietzsche's 'last people', obsessed with productive chronological time. Carolyn is fixated with social status, with career success and material acquisition. She is prepared to work tirelessly for personal achievement as an estate agent. Although determined not 'to be a victim' and to be in charge of her destiny, the film shows her enslaved to 'success' and tragically out of control.

The *kairos* of *American Beauty* is represented by a series of red symbols which resonate visually with 'the American Beauty', the red rose which lends its name to the film. Throughout the film, but predominantly in the opening scenes, every shot is framed around a red object – a bunch of roses, red lips, the Burnham's red front door, red car lights, red clothing, a red apple in the fruit bowl and – eventually – Lester's blood. The characters are arranged in tableaux around these red foci, speaking across them, looking past them, or oblivious to them hidden in the background. The red focus in each shot represents the ever-present *kairos*, the opportunity for beauty, which is possible in every moment, even death.

The person who can see most clearly the wisdom of *kairos* is Ricky, the drug-dealer, who has forsaken conventional morality in order to survive his father's regime of brutality and repression. So precious to Ricky is the beauty of the world, that he tries to preserve every moment on video tape. The 'most beautiful' of his tapes shows a white plastic bag dancing in the wind against a red brick wall. This image, which is also used to close the film, illustrates the appearance of beauty in even the most humble and ordinary of historical circumstances. This is the definitive kairic experience, the realisation of absolute beauty in an item of discarded rubbish.

Ricky also hints at the theological dimension of this *kairos*, the sense of 'a transcendent force that wanted me to know that there was no reason to be afraid . . . ever'.

Through Ricky's videos, the film is able to make a comment about the uses of art in general and cinema in particular. Ricky represents the film-maker whose mission is to draw out the hidden beauty of the world, to remind us of the kairic possibilities of life. The artist may be seen (like Ricky) as an oddball, but a few (like Lester's daughter) will recognise the truthfulness of his/her work.

American Beauty shows us the key ingredients of the post-modern *kairos*. In the first place this *kairos* is radically individualistic. Lester's precious moments are a personal album of 'Kodak moments' when the beauty of the world comes together *for him* in the passage of ordinary life. By definition, these moments are uniquely 'his' property. In the beatitude of the moment Lester is, like de Caussade's holy soul, 'solitary, free and detached from everything'. We all have our kairic experiences, but they will be private episodes locked within our personal life-stories. So life's meaning is what *you* find it to be, what *you* discover within your horizon of experience. The post-modern *kairos* does not value shared experiences and cultural histories that cannot simply be validated by personal choice. Public history cannot be determined by the individual but must be discussed, agreed and negotiated with others. The characters in the film whose self-esteem depends upon the validation of others are shown as weak and neurotic. The human ideal is a self-validating individual – which Lester becomes – who takes meaning from a radically individuated experience of time. The meaning of his life is not connected with public history or the fulfilment of civic responsibilities. What we see here is a very American and late modern individualism.

The post-modern *kairos* shows the aesthetic overcoming of ethics, the victory of the Beautiful over the Good. The ethical question of Ricky's drug business, the question of Lester's black-mailing of his employer, the question even of Lester's eventual murder are subordinated to the aesthetic question of the appearance of beauty in their lives. Lester's murder is, in the end, 'OK' because he dies with a smile on his face and a head full of beautiful memories. As Lester's corpse lies on the kitchen floor, Ricky bends down to stare at him. Ricky's gaze soaks up the beauty of the moment, utterly unfazed either by death or the violence that has caused it. *American Beauty* celebrates a radical and Nietzschean trans-valuation of values. The final arrangement of camera shots invites us to join Ricky's gaze, to look at the tragedy of death and not blink, relishing the aesthetics of death beyond the question of good and evil.

Reviewers lauded *American Beauty* as 'iconoclastic', a radical critique of the shallowness and spiritual poverty of materialism and the culture of achievement. This may be true, but the film also affirmed something deep-seated in late modern Western culture. *American Beauty* was a phenomenal success, winning five Oscars (from eight nominations), six BAFTA awards as well as numerous other accolades. Almost nobody had a bad word to say about it. Something in the film connected directly and immediately with the spirit of our age: *American Beauty* offered us a brilliant defence of the kairic philosophy of time. This was a film that made us feel *really* good, really *righteous,* about surrendering to the mysticism of Now.

Proust: *kairos* and the 'universe of convolution'

> Mystery of dustmotes playing in the sunlight.
> (Walter Benjamin, *Arcades Project*)

> In the volumes of Proust nothing happens, there is no dramatic action, there is no process. They are composed of a series of pictures extremely rich in content, but static.
> (José Ortega y Gasset, 'Time, Distance and Form in Proust')

Whatever the consolations of Kairic time, there are also problems. How do we explain the continuity between our individual moments? If life is just fragments of experience, how can we ever see what a human life looks like as a whole? Wouldn't any description of the kairic life look like a random succession of disconnected moments? This dilemma is central to the problem of writing history. History appears to be made up of distinct events, but how do all these events fit together? There is a basic tension between the integrity of each event and the pattern to which each event may belong.

Historians tend to subordinate the moments of history to the sweep of some grand narrative. The episodes of life become merely decorative, mere examples of an underlying theory of history. But life rarely, if ever, happens for us in an 'historic' way. Which of us wakes up and thinks: 'today I will be illustrating the sweep of history at the beginning of the third millennium'? We are more likely to be worrying about getting to work, or doing the shopping, or concerned for our day-to-day human relationships. We are normally blundering from event to event, doing our best to hold everything together. Our minds are not written like history books, but like scrapbooks filled with memories, present perceptions and projections into the future. Generally speaking our lives are not consciously lived as part of any 'grand plan', but are caught up in complex and multi-levelled patterns of micro events. We compile our internal sense of life-story like a photo-montage, images placed on and around each other. But with such a fragmented sense of life, where should we look to find a method of representing the overall reality of this kairic experience?

Marcel Proust is arguably the most fastidious observer of the complexity of lived experience and he is worth examining as a subtle and profound advocate of the K type view. Time is a major topic of Proust's gigantic novel *In Search of Lost Time*. And time wasn't just a literary interest: Proust was strongly influenced by Henri Bergson's philosophy of time and consciousness as a constant flow of immediate perceptions. Using some of Bergson's insights, Proust tried to write about life from the bottom up, starting from the flow of immediate perceptions and building these up into a complex narrative structure. If we want to understand how time works on the grand scale, Proust argued, we first need to take a kairic view and see time as the flow of moments.

For Proust the flux of consciousness is organised around temporal moments that he calls 'fragments of Existence withdrawn from Time'. He says elsewhere, almost metaphysically, that such a fragment 'freed from the order of time' has the power to 're-create' in us 'the man freed from the order of time.' Access to these moments is not rational, but emerges through the senses which 'bear unflinchingly, in the tiny and almost impalpable drop of their essence, the vast structure of recollection' of the past. Using this understanding of time, Proust subverts our basic expectations of narrative structure. We expect a novel to possess what Aristotle called *proairesis*, that is to say a clear and purposeful storyline. But the purpose of Proust's novel is no longer tied up with the plot or progress of the characters, still less with the realisation of the full scheme of the story. Instead the novel circulates and re-circulates around moments of experience. There is a chronology to the novel, but it has the quality of a chronicle, a list of events, a litany or ceremony. By contrast with both chronicle and plot, Proust offers another view of time as the epiphany of memory and association in what are called – even in everyday speech – 'Proustian moments'.

These moments are not so much fixed anchor points, as portals to a complex and shifting universe of memory and image. 'An image presented to us by life' says Proust, 'brings with it, in a single moment, sensations which are in fact multiple and heterogeneous.' So the exploration of our kairic experiences is a much more profound and complex process than flicking through the pages of an album of memories: 'What an abyss of uncertainty, whenever the mind feels overtaken by itself; when it, the seeker, is at the same time the dark region through which it must go seeking, and where all its equipment will avail it nothing.' But for all this uncertainty, our life's images are life-giving kairic opportunities for self-discovery and re-awakening,

> [moments] like the dress which a woman was wearing
> when we saw her for the first time, they would help me
> to re-discover the love I then had, the beauty on which
> I have superimposed so many less and less loved images,
> they would help me to find the first image again, even
> though I am no longer the 'I' who first beheld it,
> even though I must make way for the 'I' that I then was
> if that 'I' summons the thing it once knew and the 'I'
> of today does not know.

Such kairic experiences – the dress or most famously the eating of the Madeline biscuit – are all we have in Proust. The 'big picture' never comes into focus, because life is handed out in parcels of immediate, and immediately complex, experiences.

The connections between these experiences do not follow a

logical pattern that can be followed and predicted – they are not schematic, but sporadic associations of memory and fancy.

> The truth is that life is perpetually weaving fresh threads which link one individual and one event to another, and that these threads are crossed and recrossed, doubled and redoubled to thicken the web, so that any slightest point of our past and all the others a rich network of memories gives us an almost infinite variety of communicating paths to chose from.

Walter Benjamin – as we have seen, another thinker much concerned with time – calls Proust's world a 'universe of convolution' where the truth always resides in complexity. Benjamin compares Proust's achievement to that of Michelangelo's image of the creation on the ceiling of the Sistine Chapel. Both offer a cosmic image but at opposite poles of magnification: Michelangelo gives us the world as macrocosm; Proust shows us the world as a network of microcosms.

Proust's cosmic image is compiled in a way radically different from the production of a grand, organised picture. In a wonderfully self-deprecating passage Proust compares the writing of a novel to making a patchwork dress – sewing together scraps of fabric, buttons and stitching. Or pasting together pieces of paper, some torn and mended, some damaged beyond repair. Or – pushing metaphor to a comically absurd limit – making a beef stew with 'carefully chosen pieces of meat' in an enriched jelly! This haphazard process of assembly has been called 'bricolage', a useful French term for 'cobbling things together'.

What though, is the product of this bricolage? Are its components and their assembly arbitrary? Not at all, but the structure of the novel is not a system, but a dream-like constellation of elements – like the red objects in *American Beauty*. The forces that hold together the constellation are the bonds of metaphor.

> An hour is not merely an hour, it is a vase full of scents and sounds and projects and climates, and what we call reality is a certain connection between these immediate sensations and memories which envelop us simultaneously with them . . . The writer . . . can describe a

scene by describing one after another the innumerable
objects which at a given moment were present at a
particular place, but . . . truth – and life too – can be
attained by us only when, by comparing a quality
common to two sensations, we succeed in extracting
their common essence and in reuniting them to each
other, liberated from the contingencies of time, within
a metaphor.

If Proust is right, then the world can only be understood according
to an artistic logic. The links that join up the moments of life are
poetic or mythic rather than rational. The plotting of these links
results in a swirling and many-stranded narrative that cannot be
reduced to a simple system or structure. If we were to apply this
insight to a K type theology we would have to conclude that
literature is the true theology and that the telling of its story knows
no end.

There is something fabulous and beautiful about Proust's vision
of time and it is hard not to be seduced by it. But the world of our
real lives is filled not only with enchanting, meaningful or
intriguing moments, but with horror. The world is full of real
problems crying out for real solutions. The present condition of
the world is constantly begging the question of a better future.
The tragedy of the world challenges us to sacrifice some of our
present moments in the hope of better moments to come. This is
why the kairic view of time is not a fully satisfying response to
time-anxiety. The aesthetic pleasure of the moment, however
intense, does not remove either our fear of the future or our desire
for improvement. With no theory of the future at its disposal, the
K type may even take a dangerous turn towards fatalism, individualism, narcissism and irresponsibility.

The ethics of *kairos*

Tower and temple, fall to dust.
But God's power,
Hour by hour,
Is my temple and my tower.
(Robert Bridges, 'All My Hope on God is Founded')

Know the critical situation in your life
Know that it demands a decision.

(Aristotle, *Ethics*)

Behind the orgy of images something is hidden. The
world is hiding behind the profusion of images.

(Jean Baudrillard, 'Objects, Images and the
Possibilities of Aesthetic Illusion')

The K type ethic is one of 'being' rather than producing. And there
is something strongly attractive about an ethics that affirms us in
our present existence. If the past and future are not the issue we
are free to love for its own sake, giving ourselves fully to each
situation without any ulterior motive. In K time, only the present
matters, so we are not calculating the benefits of anything more
immediate than our current actions. Long term gains, pay-backs
and reciprocation are not part of the K view. In Kairic time we are
present for the other person as they are now. We are only concerned with the quality of the moment, not to change people,
persuade them or coerce them. In K time we are – potentially at
least – 'there' for the other person. This is a powerful form of
human solidarity, a complete 'being-with'.

There is also a kind of peace to be found in kairic being. Guilt
and nostalgia are left behind in the past, anxiety and ambition
belong in the future. In the pure present we are freed from 'destructive' regrets and longings. We become happy stoics, not disturbed
or resentful, not restless or uncertain, but simply abiding in the
bliss of what Virginia Woolf called our 'moments of being'.

Whatever the joys and comforts of kairic thinking – and there
are plenty of these – there are dangers too. The retreat into Kairic
time is a form of escape from public decision-making, cultural
planning, the challenge of solving problems, the demands of
justice and from public accountability. In the K type mode we are
ultimately accountable only to the moment itself and its micro
universe. As Tolle puts it in *The Power of Now*, 'there is no judgement of the Now'. The aesthetic 'fix' of each moment is sufficient
justification. Guilt about the past and anxiety about the future are
both distractions from our attentiveness to 'now'. If we are to

experience the *kairos* we must be fully available to it, fully mindful of each moment as it appears.

The kairic reaction against progressive history has been necessary and healthy. We have unsettled naïve dogmas of human self-improvement, and found new freedoms in the appreciation of life lived in the present. But the recovery of the present may be taking place at the expense of the future. The future, after all, is the future-present, a *kairos* to come. How are we to be properly responsible both to the future and to the present moment?

CHAPTER SIX

Prophetic (or P type) Time

Thy kingdom come

> No one who puts his hand to the plough, and looks
> back, is fit for the kingdom of God.
>
> (Luke 9:62)

> God is working his purpose out
> as year succeeds to year.
> God is working his purpose out
> and the time is drawing near.
>
> (A. C. Ainger, 'God is working his purpose out')

> I could weep for the criminal patience of humanity.
>
> (Samuel Taylor Coleridge)

> The moment of redemption, however secularised,
> cannot be erased from the concept [of progress].
>
> (Theodor Adorno, 'Progress')

I had to mend the garden fence last weekend. Saturday's time
suddenly took a progressive shape: a morning trip to the DIY store;
a functional lunch break; and an afternoon sinking posts and
nailing panels. These six-or-so hours were orientated towards the
completion of a job. And when the job was done, I felt good.
Saturday had been worth it, justified. Result. I hadn't simply *wasted*
time by loafing around, or *killed* it with pastimes. I had *used* time.
At the end of the day I could enjoy 'a Kit Kat moment': a mini
Sabbath, admiring my handiwork and seeing that it was good.

This was an experience of Prophetic time. It felt quite different from the expectant waiting of A type time or the aesthetic episodes of K type time. To be in P type time is to feel part of a plan – it could be a human plan, or 'the plan of nature', or 'God's plan'. The unfolding of Prophetic time feels purposeful, directed and rational. So when we wake up in the morning we are not waiting to see what the day will bring. We know already what the day is for and we get up prepared to fulfil its purpose. Most of working life is like this – task centred. P type time derives its texture and structure from the fact that there is a job in hand.

When we transpose the P type myth onto a grander scale, Prophetic time takes on a romantic and heroic character. The P type life is one spent questing after higher goals, greater achievements, new discoveries. The P type hero is one whose path of progress overcomes obstacles and enemies: she/he moulds time, creating the future rather than waiting for it. Our modern history is full of them: nation builders, social reformers, great scientists, 'historic' figures of this or that sort. They are fired by Promethean visions and dreams of the human future. Where others see tragedy, they see challenge. They embody the P type ideal: that we should give ourselves to the future as a task. Their time is driven, propelled, restless.

In religious life, the P type personality tends to turn religion into a project. The point of time is to get things done – win followers, solve problems, change society, reform abuses, improve conditions – in short, to 'make progress' of some kind. *Being* religious is not enough: religion must *produce* a better world. So the P type religious person is one who tries to organise the future, setting objectives and seeking results. This religion justifies itself in terms of things it has 'done' or 'made' or 'built'. The success of this religion is counted in identifiable achievements. So *measurement* becomes very important. P type religion will naturally tend to understand itself in terms of quantities and numbers. In order to feel good about itself, P type religion must always be able to point to increase: greater numbers of events or people, new buildings, new initiatives. But where measurable or demonstrable achievements cannot be found or produced, P type religion will feel insecure and defensive.

The idea that time can be 'managed' is central to the modern conception of Prophetic time. The 'management' of time assumes that 'time' is a resource that can be deployed in the service of specific goals. The effective 'time manager' first works out his goals and then seeks to 'use' his time in the most efficient way. Tasks are prioritised and given 'time lines' for completion. The use of time is analysed using 'activity logs' and planned using schedules. Time has a measurable, 'cost-able' value determined by the goal. Thus time becomes programmed, systematised as a means towards an end.

So Prophetic time is strongly end-orientated (eschatological) and has its centre of gravity in the future, pulling it forward. This gives it impetus and direction, but it also brings about an alienation from the present. Prophetic time tends to value the present as a utility, the point of 'now' is to serve 'then'. So a sense of the intrinsic value of the present easily gets lost. The present is always something to be overcome, something to be stood on as we reach for the future. This can create an inner feeling of loss and alienation because we are never simply 'being ourselves'. Our sense of self is always of a future self – the person we *will be* when we have achieved this or that. But we never connect with this future self, because it is always awaiting us. This sense of alienation can be deeply unsettling and draw us back into a kairic appreciation of the present or an apocalyptic appreciation of waiting. What gets lost in the prophetic calculus of time is any sense of the pleasure of time for its own sake.

Tom Hanks gives an excellent portrayal of P type time in Robert Zemeckis' film *Cast Away* (2000). Hanks plays Chuck, a manager for Federal Express, whose working life is dominated by the management of time. At the beginning of the picture there is a splendid set-piece episode where Hanks tests the FedEx parcel system by timing the delivery of a package to Moscow. When it arrives late, Chuck gives a sermon on time to the Russian workforce: 'we live or we die by the clock', he tells them. 'Relentless is our goal, relentless.' A later scene shows Chuck talking with a colleague about his wife's breast cancer. The colleague says that his wife has been advised by doctors to 'wait and see'. Chuck – unable to accept either the waiting or the tragedy of the situation – urges his friend to 'get this thing fixed', to try new treatments, and see new doctors. Chuck is simply unable to *be in the present* with his friend in his suffering. Later in the film Chuck's plane crashes and he is marooned on an isolated island. This forces a crisis in his view of

time. The crash is an event outside Chuck's control, an unmanage-
able fact that takes control of him. We see Chuck enter time in
the Catastrophic mode as he contemplates suicide. We see him
'surviving' in Apocalyptic time, awaiting rescue. We see him
painting images on rock walls in kairic acceptance of his present
situation. Finally, Chuck recovers a sense of Prophetic time. He
builds a raft and – after storms and setbacks – arrives home. The
film is a fine parable about the prophetic mode of time: its necessity
and its dangers. Before the crash, Chuck is a time control freak,
obsessed with the micro-management of inconsequential tasks. On
the island he discovers a task that really matters: his escape. The
film doesn't rubbish the Prophetic view of time, but shows that
the goals of progressive time must be linked back to real issues of
human survival and life-enhancement.

When we look at the gospels we see that Jesus had his own
human survival project: the kingdom. Jesus' teaching about the
kingdom is not only complex and ambiguous, but much-argued
over by New Testament scholars. We cannot stop to survey these
debates, but we should note that whatever *else* Jesus says about
the kingdom, he clearly saw its arrival as an apocalyptic event in
God's hands and he never gives any impression that the kingdom
can be brought about by purely human efforts. Yet Jesus also sees
human co-operation with the kingdom as important. Jesus
describes himself as 'a prophet' and his message is not only of the
impending apocalypse, but of personal ethical reform. It matters
to Jesus whether we behave like the Good Samaritan, whether we
feed the hungry and lift up the downtrodden, whether we 'bear
fruit'. Jesus' manifesto, read out in the synagogue in Nazareth
(Luke 4:16–20) describes a set of radical social transformations that
will take place in his kingdom. Jesus says that these transformations are underway even as he speaks. In other words the kingdom
is not simply something to be awaited in the Apocalyptic mode of
time. The kingdom is a developing reality in the process of arrival.
We can look forward to it, serve it, indeed, be part of it. Discipleship
doesn't just mean 'watching and praying'; it also means getting
off our knees to make real the values of the kingdom.

We have seen how, in the Letter to the Romans (see pp. 69–71
above), Paul sets out the framework of Christian Apocalyptic time.
But when we turn to the Letter to the Ephesians we find a quite

different Prophetic view of time. The church in Ephesus is urged to see itself as an organisation with a job to do. The church is not 'groaning inwardly' here. This is a church that understands its earthly mission and wants to get on with it. Whereas Paul famously saw through a glass darkly, the writer to the Ephesians has got a clear vision of the coming kingdom. The reason for this, the writer argues, is that God has 'set forth' the programme for his kingdom in the life and teachings of Christ.

> For he has made known to us in all wisdom and insight
> the mystery of his will, according to his purpose which
> he set forth in Christ as a plan for the fullness of time,
> to unite all things in him, things in heaven and things
> on earth. (Ephesians 1:10)

The Greek word for 'plan' here is *oikonomia*, from which we derive our word 'economy', implying the 'management' or 'administration' of time. How different this is from the decay and futility of human purposes that Paul spoke of in Romans. We are, according to the writer, 'created in Christ for good works' (Ephesians 2:10). We have 'boldness and confidence of access' to the divine purpose (Ephesians 3:12). This is not the apocalyptic church, huddled in waiting for the End Time. This is the prophetic church mobilised for creative participation in God's plan for the future.

The Letter to the Ephesians makes clear that the kingdom of heaven will *include* the earthly realm as we know it, uniting 'things in heaven and things in earth'. So the world we labour in will be part of the future, and our present efforts are possible contributions to the final order. This is the kind of thinking that fuels a Christianity of social transformation. Here the evangelical and liberal wings of Christianity can share a common prophetic view of time: the first believes that the world will be a better place if there are more Christians; the latter thinks that the world will be a better place if there is more practical compassion and justice. They both believe that energetic Christian work is contributing to the Big Plan.

Prophetic time and modernity

> The ultimate development of the ideal man is logically certain.
>
> (Herbert Spencer, *Social Statics*)

> The history of the world . . . presents us with a rational process.
>
> (G. W. F. Hegel, *The Philosophy of History*)

> The philosophers have only interpreted the world in various ways: the point is to change it.
>
> (Karl Marx, 'Theses on Feuerbach')

> For Christianity, history appears as the history of salvation; it then becomes the search for a worldly condition of perfection, before turning, little by little into the history of progress.
>
> (Gianni Vattimo, *The End of Modernity*)

In 1783 the German philosopher Immanuel Kant published two essays in the *Berlin Monthly:* 'Idea for a Universal History with a Cosmopolitan Purpose' and 'What is Enlightenment?' In these essays, Kant sets out the view that human history is 'the realisation of a hidden plan of nature to bring about [a] . . . perfect political constitution as the only possible state within which all natural capacities of mankind can be developed completely'. Kant's essays are significant because they crystallise a conviction that was prevalent in the later eighteenth century: the belief in secular historical progress. This wasn't so much an empirical conclusion drawn from the observation of human affairs. It was essentially a form of faith: a non-rational conviction about the nature of human time.

Kant was not a dewy-eyed optimist and he recognised the human C type potential. He believed that human nature was 'crooked timber', and that nothing man-made could ever be perfect. However, humans are also rational, said Kant, and being rational they will in due course build for themselves the best possible form of social organisation. Along the way there will be 'devastations', 'upheavals', 'folly' and 'caprice' – but in the end humans will choose to 'take the step which reason could have suggested to them without so many sad experiences'. Eventually, Kant prophesied, there would be a great world 'federation of peoples'. All humanity would live in freedom and there would be no more wars.

These views may not seem strange to us now, but this was a new way of thinking. Peter Gay, the historian of the Enlightenment, describes it as 'a great reorientation' in our thinking about time. In the Renaissance people had looked to the past for their inspiration: to Plato and Aristotle and the great classical authors. But with the emergence of modern science, time took a one-eighty turn: people started to think in terms not of past glories, but future possibilities. The shape of tomorrow appeared to be in our hands and as such we could design and engineer our own future. With this reorientation, human time shifted decisively into the P type mode. The point of being human was now to *produce* the future, to imagine the best kind of human society and then work towards it. Under the creed of historical progress, the meaning of human life was to be useful and productive.

The continuing scientific and social achievements of nineteenth- and twentieth-century Europe provided – for those who were looking for it – endless 'proof' of the progressive path of Western history. Previously fatal diseases became treatable, new rights and freedoms were enshrined in law, education and healthcare became accepted as basic entitlements. These achievements seemed to point to something more than just a run of good fortune, or a one-off 'age of improvement'. It felt, in Kant's view, that humanity was growing up, shrugging off its immaturity and stepping out into an entirely new and irreversible epoch of progress.

Many historians of ideas – and most notably Rudolf Bultmann and Karl Löwith – have argued that Kant's conception of history as 'the realisation of a hidden plan of nature' is a secular version of the eschatological plan referred to in Ephesians. This is the so-called 'secularisation thesis', the suggestion that there is a hidden theology at the heart of modernism. At the very moment when European culture thought it was leaving God behind, it was in fact merely hiding God away in a secular understanding of history as a planned process of improvement and human growth. The names had changed, but the creature was basically still the same. God's plan had become 'the plan of nature'. The plan once revealed by God in scripture was now revealed by 'reason'. The desire to serve God had become a desire to serve 'humanity'. The saviour was once a divine person, now human beings would 'save them-selves'. But, fundamentally, the view of time still remained staunchly prophetic.

The person who articulated this hidden theology most power-fully was the nineteenth-century German philosopher Georg Hegel. Hegel argued that all history is a working out of rational processes. The force pushing these processes on was something Hegel called *Geist*, which is translated both as 'spirit' and 'mind'. In essence *Geist* is human freedom, and all historical forces push in the direction of the realisation of this freedom. Hegel believed that in its original state human society consisted of a series of tensions, oppositions and divisions of power. In this state humans were oppressive and oppressed, fearful and unfulfilled. History is the process by which these oppositions play themselves out – often in bloody conflict, warfare and revolutions – reconfiguring human society until it reaches an 'end of history' in which all the tensions are held together in a dynamic but peaceful and stable system. In this state everyone is as free as they possibly can be. The arrival of this system – what we now call 'liberal democracy' – would be heaven on earth, the concrete realisation of human freedom in a set of laws and cultural practices. Liberal democracy is, for Hegel, God's own political economy. It may not *look* religious but, as Hegel argued in his lectures on the philosophy of history, 'secular life . . . is the positive and definitive embodiment of the Spiritual Kingdom'. So when you next cast your vote in the local elections, or avail yourself of your right to a hearing about your parking ticket, or feel safe in your home because you know that the police are patrolling the area – all this is the happening of God's kingdom. Just being a free citizen is a spiritual condition. So God's kingdom is not a wispy realm of harp-strumming angels, but a concrete world of real people living in freedom and justice.

Hegel believed that Christianity had grasped all this in the concept of God as Holy Spirit. Hegel saw the Holy Spirit as 'picture language' for his more philosophical concept of *Geist*. With the idea of the Holy Spirit, Christianity had understood that God is incarnated into social interactions and processes. The Holy Spirit binds the Christian community together and guides it through time, rather as *Geist* directs all human history towards its future. So the Holy Spirit is a way of speaking about divine rationality or the mind of God. In time the mind of God slowly becomes a living and breathing reality in human history. So time is fundamentally providential: we just have to read the newspapers to see God working his purpose out.

However, Hegel had little time for what he called the 'piddling' view of providence: the superstitious belief that God intervenes here and there to protect or benefit 'the god squad'. Hegel's idea of providence was akin to that expressed in Ephesians. Providence is the implementation of a plan for all things in heaven and earth, a plan operating in every second of every human life, whether explicitly Christian or not. Every rational person can *see* that history is providential because the evolving human system of laws and rights *is* the divine plan. Moreover, reason allows us to intuit the idea of the perfect state, prophetically, before it becomes a reality. We can *think the future* before it is externalised as a state of affairs. So Hegel sees the movement of history as the 'progression from the abstract to the concrete', that's to say from the 'plan' to the 'fullness of time'.

Hegel's theory of history was adopted by others – such as Windischmann and Weisse – as the inspiration for a new Christian activism. Hegel's philosophy gave Christian ethics a whole new field of operation. Being ethical in Hegelian Christianity was not just a matter of doing 'good deeds' or being 'a good person', but about creating and transforming human institutions. Christian philanthropists sought not only to alleviate suffering, but to make structural changes that would eliminate suffering permanently. They built schools and hospitals, set up welfare organisations, and some even constructed complete model towns. In short, they believed that Christians should take the lead in designing a society free from unhappiness and ignorance. In urban areas in particular, the church became a symbol of social progress, a sign that better times were on the way. Henry Walker's survey of 'Christian Work and Workers' in London's East End (1869) noted

> . . . the buoyancy of the rising tide and the energy of the younger life. New and imposing buildings, educational,

religious and charitable, everywhere meet the eye. The great . . . plain of East London is thickly set with towers and spires and hospitable beacons stretching still farther and farther East to the far Essex beyond. They rise like lighthouses from the once dreary swamp or the cheerless highway, telling of newer forces and helpful centres now available for a hardly-pressed people.

This is a world away from St Paul awaiting the apocalypse or T. S. Eliot musing on the convergence of all time on the present. This is time that knows where it is going and cannot wait to get there.

There is something wonderfully inspiring about the vision of Prophetic time, whether in Ephesians or in Hegel's philosophy of history. It feels good to be part of some greater purpose. Not only do our days take meaning from a connection with a plan of history, but our whole lives feel justified. And which of us has not looked at the world and thought: we *could* change this place if we wanted, we *could* eliminate poverty, war, hunger and disease? And if we *could*, wouldn't the world look at least a little bit like heaven? And wouldn't the realisation of that world be something worth working for and sacrificing for? Plenty have dreamed such dreams. Plenty have pressed their shoulders to the wheel of historical progress. But for all their efforts, the kingdom of heaven on earth still looks a long way off. And even the staunchest believer in progress must wonder at times whether we will ever get there.

Tragedy and progress

Progress has atrophied in us all that is spiritual.

(Charles Baudelaire, *Intimate Journals*)

History may not manifestly be revealed as the theatre of a directing purpose on earth – of which our shallow histories boast so much – for we may not be able to espy its final end. But it may conceivably offer us glimpses of a divine theatre through the openings and ruins of individual scenes.

(J. F. Herder, *Yet Another Philosophy of History*)

> Conversation in its primary form is an exploration of
> possibilities in the search for truth.
>
> (David Tracy, *Plurality and Ambiguity*)

One of the great mysteries of the human condition is that despite knowing what is good for us, we often do not act in our own best interests. I know that I *ought* to take more exercise and cut back my consumption of chocolate. I know it would be good for me. But I don't act on this knowledge. This is very strange. I am after all a rational creature and can see the foolishness of my actions. If we know what is good for us, why on earth don't we do it? This is not only an individual problem. We can all think what an ideal world would look like – at least in its fundamentals – so why haven't we built such a world? Why has historical progress been so haphazard? Why so painfully slow?

One answer is to put the failure of progress down to a defect in human nature: history *would* progress if it were not for human perversity. Aristotle had such a theory, arguing that humans suffer from *akrasia* or 'weakness'. Christianity, famously, said that all humans were pre-conditioned with a moral defect called 'original sin'. Freud – as we have seen – argued that we all posses a destructive 'death drive' which undermines all civilising projects. But what if the problem did not lie with human nature, but with the very concept of progressive time itself? This would mean that there is a basic flaw in our culture of progress and civilisation. In other words, pure progressive time is corrupt and will always also involve regression.

Probably the most celebrated critique of progressive history was made by Max Horkheimer and Theodor Adorno in a book called *The Dialectic of Enlightenment* first published in 1944. Adorno and Horkheimer argued that the emergence of the Third Reich was not just an aberration or setback in the progress of civilisation, but was a direct product of a progressive view of history. Fascism was one way of expressing the idea that we can organise time into a planned programme.

The problem lay with the very idea of a 'plan' for enlightenment. Once there is a plan, this must be implemented, and resources for the plan must be controlled and managed. Those who do not agree with the plan or who do not co-operate with it must also be 'managed'. The whole project of bringing about a planned future requires the imposition of what Adorno and Horkheimer call 'instrumental reason': a controlling rationality, which presses all of nature in service to its chosen goals. So even when the goal of progress is human freedom, the mechanism of progress will require some kind of coercion: as Adorno and Horkheimer put it in one of their many slogans: 'the power of progress involves the progress of power'.

Adorno and Horkheimer saw progressive time as a 'myth' based upon a cluster of illusions: the illusion of human power over nature; the illusion that 'reason' is an innocent faculty that always directs us towards freedom; the illusion that the progress of history is both benevolent and necessary. Adorno saw modern history as the very opposite of progress – as *Zufallsgeschichte*, or a 'history of decay'. 'No [progressive] history leads from savagery to humanitarianism,' argued Adorno, 'but there is one from the slingshot to the megaton bomb.' Adorno had no faith at all in human progress, indeed he thought that the very idea of progress was dangerous. The minute we form ideas of progress we also give birth to ideas of control and power. So Adorno recommended a radical suspicion of all P type time, and a radical critique of power that he called 'the negative dialectic'.

The cultural problems with progressive time can also be experienced at the personal level, and with tragic consequences. I joined the Army when I left school. It was a great outlet for youthful male energy and my love of gadgets. It also felt good to be part of a team with a mission. I felt absorbed into what felt like a greater and higher task, something noble and worth making sacrifices for. Time in the Army wasn't always progressive – vast swathes of time were spent in waiting and preparation. But time was essentially conceived in prophetic terms: there was a job to do, a mission to execute. The Army loved to use a vocabulary of improvement: better, bigger, stronger, faster, more efficient and so on. Many people love this culture and find a powerful sense of security in being part of a corporate plan. But it wasn't for everyone. Someone who joined before me had – so I heard – shot himself through the temple by loading his rifle with a blank round and dropping a pencil down the barrel. He had felt traumatised and oppressed by the scheme of Army life and saw no way out.

When we are in control of its purpose or feel inspired by the task, P type time can feel good. But the flip side of P time is *oppression*. When a task is imposed upon us, when we don't believe in it, when the task inhibits our freedom, P time is experienced as enslavement. The slave's time may look busy and purposeful from the outside. But the slave is alienated from her own time. Her time, as we say, is not her own. The slave's life certainly has a purpose, but it is a purpose without any personal meaning. Working time can often have the feeling of enslavement: when, for example, we do not really believe in what we are doing, but do not feel free to escape. The task – however clear and organised – becomes oppressive, meaningless and destructive. At this point Prophetic time turns into Catastrophic time. Time possesses the *form* of Prophetic time, but is *experienced* in a catastrophic way.

Progressive time always has this potential to oppress, to insist on uniformity. This is why Adorno was so wary of ideologies of progress. He thought we should always be suspicious of those with schemes for a better world. Plans require power and power is inherently dangerous. Adorno's worries about progress were not just academic. Many have died in the name of 'progress', and who can doubt that many more will?

But something more sinister still has happened to the ideology of progress in our culture. The visible failure of so-called 'enlightened' Western nations to solve problems and create a better world has generated a deep cynicism about ideas of historical progress. This has created a strong interest in kairic and apocalyptic views of time. If we cannot plan effectively for the future, let us at least find meaning elsewhere: say, in the beauty of the present moment or the stillness of empty waiting time. However, the rhetoric of progress is still a strong feature of our life. We want better cars, faster computers, better communication and so on. But these 'progressive' desires are not connected to any general vision of the future. We no longer really know what progress is for. We are surrounded by the trappings of progress and images of improvement, but without any plans or objectives. We experience 'progressive time' merely as acquisition or addition. So we have the constant *feeling* of progression – new developments, new technologies, new fashions – without any theory about the direction, purpose or even of the value of progress.

Looking at our culture from the outside, one could be forgiven for thinking that we have never been so obsessed with Prophetic time. We regulate our time with an ever-increasing control and urgency. We are busy, busy people. But busy doing what exactly? Being busy has almost become a pursuit in its own right, a natural good. We no longer have to ask whether our business is in service to any noble purpose. It just feels good to be busy. We feel justified.

This is, in effect, the collapse of Prophetic time into a Kairic mode. This new kind of Prophetic time has become a way of experiencing the present without having to take any responsibility for the future. When I at last get my hands on a plasma screen TV, I will have the sensation of having 'progressed'. But this 'progress' is really all to do with the gratification of a kairic impulse to enjoy the present moment. My plasma screen TV will not have contributed anything to the public future. Everywhere now we are invited to 'consume' and call it 'progress'.

This begs many questions. We should ask ourselves who is in control of this direction-less progressive time. Are we in charge of it? Or are we enslaved to it? We should also ask what happened to the old dreams of progress. Are these now redundant? Do we indeed have any real sense at all of the long-term future? When we think a hundred years ahead, what if anything do we dream of and what do we desire? These questions also need to be asked within the churches. Does the church now have any progressive dream of its own future? Have we abandoned long-term plans in favour of an apocalyptic philosophy of 'let's wait and see'? Are we seeking security in a kairic philosophy of neither toiling nor spinning, but living for the day? Does it matter any longer whether the church has an image of its ideal future? What now is the role of progressive time in late modern ecclesial life?

These are not easy questions to answer. Simple dreams of an ideal future can look naïve and unrealistic. We'd all 'like to teach the world to sing in perfect harmony' as the Coca Cola advert put it. But mere visions do not tell us how to solve the intractable human problems that stand in the way. A meaningful theory of progress would have to explain the *mechanisms* of historical progress. Furthermore, all dreams of the future emerge from particular cultural settings. The Christian view of 'perfect harmony' may not harmonise with the Muslim view, or the view of free-market economics. A practical vision of a harmonic world future would have to allow for many cultural differences.

So progressive time must now take the form of a conversation. Progressive time can no longer be the experience of seeing one's own plan prevail. It is felt rather as the development of consensus about the shape of a plan. To be engaged in progressive time is to find oneself talking – with others – about the future. The plan is not the work of one controlling rationality, but the product of many minds, many experiences, many cultures.

Over the past 50 years the German philosopher Jürgen Habermas has been at the forefront of thinking about 'conversation' and 'communication' as the basis of a progressive view of history. Habermas has called for the development of 'communicative practice' – that's to say the art of conversation across cultural and social divisions.

Habermas recognises all of Adorno's fears about progress. But unlike Adorno, Habermas still believes in the importance of making a better future and solving human problems. Habermas argues that we must give up the old enlightenment ideal of a grand plan for history. Instead we must commit ourselves to a new ideal: the ideal of serious dialogue with others about what the future should be. So instead of trying to describe what the *perfect world* would look like we should try to understand what the *perfect conversation* would look like. The new P type project would not be the implementation of a master plan, but a careful negotiation with others through time.

Imagine the perfect conversation, says Habermas. Everyone would be allowed to have his or her say. People would not only listen to other points of view, but seek to understand them. No one would be shouted down or frozen out. Conversational partners would seek out common languages and a shared understanding of reason. All the partners to the conversation would seek to include all the others. Habermas calls this 'the ideal speech situation' – an impossible (or at least improbable) state of affairs, but a useful ideal. We should seek to promote the conditions of ideal speech, not so much as an end in itself but as the mechanism for moving forwards in time. The ideal speech situation is an ethic of progress.

The theologian David Tracy has followed Habermas in

recommending conversation as the basis for historical progress. Tracy sees conversation as a game with 'hard rules':

> Say only what you mean; say it as accurately as you can; listen to and respect what the other says, however different or other; be willing to correct or defend your opinions if challenged by a conversational partner; be willing to argue if necessary, to confront if demanded, to endure necessary conflict, to change your mind if the evidence suggests it.

The point of the conversation is neither kairic nor apocalyptic, but definitely progressive. The reason for the conversation is not to pass the time or to bring pleasure, but to make historical headway. But the outcome of the conversation has not been sealed in advance. This is open progress, progress as adventure, progress as faith.

This may seem a world away from the 'plan' in Ephesians. But perhaps we need to look again at what the writer to the Ephesians says about the 'divine plan'. At the centre of the plan are very particular standards of human relations, including 'hard rules' about how we should speak to one another. In fact the writer to the Ephesians recommends an ethic of conversation that would raise few protests from Habermas or Tracy. The essence of conversation is that we should 'speak the truth in love':

> Therefore, putting away falsehood, let everyone speak the truth with his neighbour, for we are members one of another. (Ephesians 4:25)

These are important words for any culture – within the church or without – which is seeking in late modern times to understand the journey to its own future.

CONCLUSION

I should have ordered the chicken

> There are many different logics, and not just a single logic. This means that no single logic is strong enough to support the total construction of human knowledge.
>
> (Jean Piaget, *Principles of Genetic Epistemology*)

> Time is not a line, but a network of intentionalities.
>
> (Maurice Merleau-Ponty, *Phenomenology of Perception*)

> For life to be large and full, it must contain the care of past and of the future in every passing moment of the present.
>
> (Emilia Gould in Joseph Conrad's *Nostromo*)

I'm one of those people who always regret what they've ordered in a restaurant. I'll choose a steak and when it comes, I'll wish I'd ordered the chicken like my wife. If I order the chicken, I'll regret not having the steak. If I'm too tormented by my wrong choice, she's often gracious enough to swap.

It's an obvious but important truth that every choice we make in life involves the sacrifice of other options. We can't have it all. Your decision to read this book, for example, means that some other book will not get read. When we choose something we also reject other possibilities. This simple fact has profound conse-quences because good ethical choices can only take place by sacrificing other good ethical choices: a pound given to famine relief is a pound not given to cancer research.

This dilemma was portrayed poignantly in *Sophie's Choice* (1982, dir: Alan J. Pakula), where a mother, Sophie (played by Meryl Streep), is forced to decide which of her two children to save. Her choice is double-edged, rescuing one child will mean that the other will die. This is a special and appalling case of the situation that prevails for all of us: when you choose something, you lose something.

The way we deal with time is also a kind of choice. We may not make this choice deliberately, indeed we may not even realise that a choice has been made. But whichever way we live out our time – in the C, A, K or P mode – we will have 'chosen' one possibility and excluded others. This is just how it goes. It's not possible to give oneself to an epiphany in the present *and* be labouring for future goals. Waiting excludes purposeful activity and vice versa. We can't be in all the modes of time at once any more than we can simultaneously be in Birmingham and Brighton.

Clearly we do switch in and out of the different modes of time depending upon the circumstances. Art and liturgy require kairic attentiveness to the ongoing present. Uncertainty about the future requires waiting. Tasks, jobs and chores require a purposeful approach to time. But these shifts are merely functional and take place against the backdrop of a basic preference for one mode of time over the others. Deep down each of us will feel that the *essence of time* is Catastrophic, *or* Kairic, *or* Apocalyptic *or* Prophetic.

Someone might object that there is no need for an underlying view of time. Can't we just shift in and out of the various modes of time as the occasion demands without believing that time has any deep structure? However, it is not so easy to dispense with a deep view of time: the idea that there is no underlying structure of time is in fact strongly kairic because it sees time as a sequence of 'occasions'. We can't get away from it: we do have a deep-down view about what time is. And in taking this view we have excluded the alternatives.

In our current post-modern age, the Apocalyptic and Kairic modes of time are the most congenial to us. We feel safe and reassured by the popular wisdom that what really matters is 'the power of now'. We have fetishised 'immediacy' in the concept of 'real time'. We have replaced future planning with the defensive management of risks and fear of risks. Our capacity and willingness to imagine and create the future is diminished. We expect to endure problems rather than to solve them. The ideal future, the heavenly city, no longer exists powerfully in our contemporary imagination. We are, in sum, simply at risk of losing sight of the future. This exclusion of the prophetic mode is a concern, and the recovery of a faith in Prophetic time – perhaps understood, as I have suggested, as an open process of dialogue – should be a cultural priority.

The church in general, or a church locally, should reckon what is gained and lost by giving preference to any one view of time. The strongly P type church will be a productive organisation busy with projects and schemes. Being part of such a church will give a feeling of purpose and mission, but will such a church find a way of valuing what is simply beautiful but unproductive? Will such a church be properly open to others, or will it see them functionally in relation to its task? By contrast the K type church will be a reflective organisation which values events and human encounters for their own sake. But such a church will perhaps have sacrificed a strong sense of the Christian mission (however conceived). The A type church may take a number of forms, but will possibly be busy but defensive. This church will be an upholder of traditions and practices; its task will be to survive the perceived risks to its doctrines and habits. Such a church may profit from engaging with the future in a more creative way, and from a more open attitude to the opportunities (rather than the threats) of contemporary culture.

If an 'ideal' view of time were possible, it would perhaps take the form of a combination of the modes of time. But we are in chalk and cheese territory here and a tidy combination is not possible. What is possible, however, is a way of living with tensions, of counting the cost of the possibilities we reject. So the prophetic movers and shakers need to hold on to the need to value the present; those disposed to see life as waiting need to hold on to the importance of solving problems and building futures; those who venerate 'moments of being' need also to understand moments of becoming. We need, somehow, to live *within* the grid of conflicting modes of time.

The qualities required to live like this are an openness to alternative perspectives and the ability to live with paradox. We need the ability to hold open contradictory time-views and not to be fazed by the tension. Time is not simple, but a complex space in which different attitudes coexist. There is no 'simple' version of what time is for us. Anyone who offers a 'simple' meaning has merely blocked off other valid possibilities.

The complexity of time should not be seen as a problem, but as a positive quality of abundance and richness. Our experience of time is complex because it is full of possibilities and alternatives. The Bible has a word for this feeling of richness: *pleroma*, which is translated mostly as 'fullness'. The *pleroma* cannot be experienced as a simple sensation or idea: it is the complex, layered, fluid, lived duration of human existence in all its modes and possibilities. To be aware of this complexity is not problematic and difficult, but exhilarating and liberating.

It is the task of a good philosophy or theology to provide us with the intellectual tools to understand both the richness of time-experience, and our own time preferences. Moreover, philosophy enables us to evaluate and assess the choices we have made, giving us the capacity to modify or change our attitudes. Philosophical reflection permits us to offer a critique of our preferred type of time, and gives us a better understanding of its value. Philosophy holds open the field of choices, like a menu, allowing us to see both what we have chosen and what we have sacrificed.

But philosophy and theology cannot tell us which choice is ultimately 'right', because there is no ultimately 'right' choice. Time, as we have seen, is not anything known. We cannot check our preferences against the 'official' meaning of time. We understand time from *within* cultural myths about its meaning. If we want to evaluate our choice of myth we must use other means of validation: we must ask which type of time best fits our experience, which makes us most happy, which makes life most bearable, beautiful and satisfying. That's as close to 'ultimately right' as we can get. But our choices do not get rubber stamped from above. We choose them and we must live with them.

However, we do not have to live with blind choice. If philosophy has one basic, non-negotiable prejudice, it is the presupposition that understanding is better than ignorance. This does not mean that we can understand everything, but it does mean that it is better to be aware of our ignorance, than to be *both* ignorant *and* oblivious to our ignorance. A philosophy of time enables us to understand that time is lived in different modes, that these modes are chosen, and that all our choices involve the sacrifice of alternatives. But philosophy cannot make the choice for us.

This does not mean that our choices do not matter, or that any choice is as good as any other. Our philosophy of time matters deeply – it can bring us happiness or despair, it can redeem us from time-anxiety or leave us fretful about the meaning of our lives. It's like the choice of who to love, or who to have as our friends. As W. H. Auden put it, 'Time is our choice of How to love and Why'. It is a 'life-decision' that could hardly be more important. Our philosophy of time can heal or destroy. But by its nature, this choice is always particular to a person or a culture.

Time's up

> Time passes.
> That is all.
> Make sense who may.
> I switch off.
>
> (Samuel Beckett, What Where)

How do you end a book on time? It's taken me fifty thousand minutes of writing time to get to this point – that's roughly 833 hours or 35 days. That's 0.13 per cent of my life. Let's suppose that you read at a rate of about 5000 words an hour. This book will have taken up about 10 hours of your life – assuming that you've read the book from cover to cover. Everything in life can be subjected to the calculus of time. That's because our lives are time. You and I are an allocation of hours and minutes. That's why a philosophy of time is essential. Don't let anyone tell you that philosophy is irrelevant or merely academic. Philosophy – if it's done properly – is a survival discipline.

So – if it's not a rude question – what's your philosophy of time?

Let me imagine you now, drifting away from me. You know me after a fashion, but frankly, I have no idea who you are or when you are. You could be anyone at any time. Sure, I care who you are. And I care what you think about the ideas in this book. I care what you think about time. That's why I've invested 35 days in this book. But now it is late. It is now midnight on 25 June 2003.

I've written what I have written and the asymmetry of time means that I can't take it back again.

BIBLIOGRAPHICAL NOTES

This is not a comprehensive bibliography on the philosophy and theology of time, but a personal selection of books from which I drew ideas or inspiration. For more comprehensive information please see the anthologies on the philosophy of time mentioned at the end of these notes. For anyone who would value suggestions for further reading, I have tried to give a few helpful recommendations.

Prologue

Bergson's philosophy of time is set out in a book called *Duration and Simultaneity* first published in 1922 (Clinamen Press, 1999). Chapter 3, 'Concerning the Nature of Time' describes the key ideas. This chapter along with many other useful texts can be found in Charles M. Sherover's excellent anthology *The Human Experience of Time* (Northwestern University Press, 2001).

One of the title quotations is taken from Alexandre Kojève's *Introduction to the Reading of Hegel* (Cornell University Press, 1980). Although this book will only really be of interest to serious readers of Hegel, Kojève had a great influence on Francis Fukuyama who used Kojève's interpretation of Hegel in his book *The End of History and the Last Man* (Penguin, 1993). Fukuyama has been much criticised but I think he has initiated a very important debate about the nature of human progress.

'Wittgenstein's ladder' is a reference to the remarkable last paragraph of his *Tractatus Logico-Philosophicus* (Routledge, 2001). 'My propositions serve as elucidations in the following way: anyone who understands them eventually recognizes them as nonsensical, when he has used them – as steps – to climb up beyond them. (He must, so to speak, throw away the ladder after he has climbed up it.)'

Introduction

At the top of this chapter I quote from two authors who have had a great influence on me: Italo Calvino and Frank Kermode. Calvino's fiction is deliciously playful and witty. The first thing I read by him is still my favourite: *If on a Winter's Night a Traveller* (Vintage, 1992) – a novel that keeps starting but never properly gets going. Calvino's *Six Memos for the Next Millennium* (Vintage, 1996) is thought-provoking and I took some ideas from the final essay on 'multiplicity'. Frank Kermode's *The Sense of an Ending* (OUP, 1968) is a classic study of literature and eschatology, with many wonderful reflections

131

on time. Kermode's *The Genesis of Secrecy* (Harvard University Press, 1979) is the most inspiring book I have ever read on biblical interpretation.

St Augustine's argument that all apparent flaws in creation are the 'privation' of God's beauty and goodness can be found in *City of God* (CUP, 1998) Book VII, chapters 1–8. In Book XIII of *Confessions* (tr. Maria Boulding, Hodder & Stoughton, 1999), Augustine affirms at length the coherence and goodness of every created thing.

Paul Ricoeur is best read through his essays. His 3–volume *Time and Narrative* (University of Chicago Press, 1990) is far too long and should be read very selectively. *History and Truth* (Northwestern, 1965) is a collection of interesting early essays. *Figuring The Sacred* (Fortress Press, 1995) contains an essay on 'Biblical Time', along with many other theological pieces.

James Barr's *Biblical Words for Time* (SCM Press, 1962) is really a book about biblical interpretation, but contains many useful observations about the biblical lexicon for time and how lexical analysis should be used. Other useful texts are: Henri Yaker, 'Time in the Biblical and Greek Worlds' in Yaker et al, *The Future of Time* (Anchor Books, 1972) and J. F. Callahan, *Four Views of Time in Ancient Philosophy* (Harvard University Press, 1948).

Here is a selection of Christian books on the theology of time: J. Marsh, *The Fulness of Time* (Nisbet, 1952); John Robinson, *In the End God* (James Clarke & Co, 1950); Oscar Cullman, *Christ and Time* (Westminster Press, 1949); Paul Fiddes, *The Promised End* (Blackwell, 2000); William Lane Craig, *Time and Eternity: Exploring God's Relationship with Time* (Crossway, 2001); Craig C. Hill, *In God's Time*, (Eerdmans, 2002).

Hayden White is the clearest and most interesting of the narrativist philosophers of history. If you can't face White's 450–page *Metahistory* (Johns Hopkins, 1973) help is at hand in a 30–page essay that summarises his argument: 'Interpretation in History' in Hayden White, *Tropics of Discourse* (Johns Hopkins, 1978). Northrop Frye writes about narrativism from a Christian perspective: see *The Great Code* (Harvest, 1981), *The Double Vision* (University of Toronto Press, 1991) and *The Anatomy of Criticism* (Princeton University Press, 2000) in which he sets out a four-fold narrative classification.

The Deconstruction of Time

Chapter XI of St Augustine's *Confessions* is essential reading for anyone interested in the theology or philosophy of time. Augustine's arguments against circular models of history can be found in *City of God*, Book XII, chapters 10–21.

The poems of St John of the Cross are an accessible way into his thought (*Poems of St John of the Cross*, tr. Roy Campbell, Collins, 1979). 'Verses written after an ecstasy of high exaltation' describes an encounter with God where St John finds himself without words or knowledge: 'the further I climbed the height, the less I seemed to understand'. There are a number of studies of St John, including E. Allison Peers, *Spirit of Flame: A Study of St John of the Cross* (SCM Press, 1947). A good selection of Meister Eckhart's writings can be found in *The Wisdom of Meister Eckhart* (Grail Publications, 2003). For a study of

Eckhart see Robert K. Foreman, *Meister Eckhart: The Mystic as Theologian* (Element Books, 1991) and Bruce Milem, *The Unspoken Word* (Catholic University of America, 2002). Angelus Silesius' classic work is *Cherubinic Wanderer* (SPCK, 1986). *The Cloud of Unknowing* is available as a 'Penguin Classic' (2001) or (if you can find it second hand) along with other 14th-century mystical writings in Karen Armstrong (ed.), *The English Mystics* (Kyle Cathie, 1991).

Rowan Williams shows himself deeply sympathetic to negative theology in *Open to Judgement* (Darton, Longman & Todd, 1994) which has half a dozen essays on the theme of the 'unknown god'. For a more radical study see George Pattison's *Agnosis: Theology in the Void* (Macmillan, 1996). Pattison shows that the theme of 'unknowing' is strongly present in Eastern as well as Western religious traditions. Robert E. Carter (ed.), *God, the Self and Nothingness* (Continuum, 1990), is a collection of essays looking at the use of 'the negative' in Eastern and Western religion.

Derrida's writing is a major challenge for the non-specialist reader – it is very densely written and laden with jargon and philosophical references. Christopher Norris has written two good, clear introductions to Derrida's philosophy: *Deconstruction: Theory and Practice* (Methuen, 1986) and *Derrida* (Fontana, 1987). A general description of Derrida's deconstruction can also be found in the introduction to my *Impossible God: Derrida's Theology* (Ashgate, 2003). The opening sections of *Of Grammatology* (Johns Hopkins, 1998) are a good place to start reading Derrida's own writings. Edmund Husserl's work is best approached through his *Paris Lectures* (Nijhoff, 1975) or the *Encyclopaedia Britannica* (14th edition, vol. 17, 1929) article on 'Phenomenology', which was written by Husserl himself. There is a wealth of secondary literature on Husserl, but the best short introduction I know of is Leszek Kolakowski's *Husserl and the Search for Certitude* (University of Chicago Press, 1987).

Zeno's arguments can be found in Kirk and Raven, *The Presocratic Philosophers* (CUP, 1974). McTaggart's argument that time is not real is reproduced in Le Poidevin and MacBeath (eds), *The Philosophy of Time* (OUP, 1993) along with other essays from the analytic tradition of philosophy, including Michael Dummett's fascinating piece 'Bringing about the Past'. Spinoza is very difficult to read from cold. I would suggest reading either Stuart Hampshire's *Spinoza* (Penguin, 1988) or Roger Scruton's *Spinoza* (OUP, 1986) before turning to the *Ethics* (Penguin, 1996) or other works.

Catastrophic Time

I took the idea of the 'horror of history' from Mircea Eliade. Although Eliade has some very profound ideas I have never found his books either very enjoyable or easy to read. However, two books were particularly helpful, *Cosmos and History* (Princeton University Press, 1991) and *Myth and Reality* (Harper and Row, 1963).

Donne's Easter Day sermon on re-compacted bodies can be found in *John Donne*, John Carey (ed.) (The Oxford Authors, OUP, 1990). The eschatological implications of the Eucharist are drawn out by Geoffrey Wainwright in

Eucharist and Eschatology (OUP, 1981). Edward Young's *Night Thoughts* (Dover Publications, 1976) is readily available second hand in a variety of editions.

Volume 12 of the Pelican Freud Library contains both 'Civilization and its Discontents' and the exchange of letters between Freud and Einstein (Penguin, 1991). Norman O. Brown's *Life Against Death, The Psychoanalytical Meaning of History* (Sphere, 1959) is an interesting application of Freud's drive theory to the philosophy of history. I found Brown's analysis of death, time and anxiety particularly insightful (Chapter 8, 'Death, Time and Eternity').

Georges Bataille's *Literature and Evil* (Marion Boyars, 1985) is a very accessible book and contains his essay on de Sade, along with pieces on Proust, Kafka and others. Bataille's *Theory of Religion* (Zone Books, 1992) is a more difficult read, but I found it worth the effort.

I am still trying to absorb properly what Slavoj Žižek is saying, and whether I really agree with him. But he certainly provokes thought, and I found two books particularly interesting: *The Fragile Absolute – or, why the Christian legacy is worth fighting for* (Verso, 2000) and *On Belief* (Routledge, 2001). These books argue that 'the Christian legacy is much too precious to be left to the fundamentalist freaks'. Žižek admires the Christian emphasis upon personal decision. The Christian must make a 'primordial choice' to *change* him/herself in the name of a higher cause or calling. So Christians do not merely 'discover' their true selves, they change into their true selves through a process of personal critique and transformation. It is this possibility of human change – and therefore of historical change – that Žižek sees as the basis of hope.

Terry Eagleton's recent study of the tragic consciousness *Sweet Violence: The Idea of the Tragic* (Blackwell, 2003) offers an interesting argument for the value of tragedy as the state of consciousness that inspires desire, revolution and transformation. Oliver Bennet's *Cultural Pessimism* (Edinburgh University Press, 2001) analyses some of the themes of the post-modern sense of decline. Arthur Herman looks at cultural pessimism in a more general way in *The Idea of Decline in Western History* (The Free Press, 1997).

Apocalyptic Time

The literature on apocalyptic thinking, in the Bible and beyond, is vast. Frances Carey (ed.), *The Apocalypse and the Shape of Things to Come* (British Museum Press, 1999) contains good essays on a range of themes from the biblical origins of the apocalyptic tradition to apocalypse in cinema. Craig C. Hill's *In God's Time* (Eerdmans, 2002) gives a good and accessible account of the biblical tradition. John Collins, *The Apocalyptic Imagination* (Eerdmans, 1998) is an introduction to Jewish apocalyptic literature. The first theologian to argue that Jesus was essentially a radical apocalyptic prophet was Albert Schweitzer in his *The Quest of the Historical Jesus* (SCM Press, 2000). Schweitzer said that in the eighteenth and nineteenth centuries there was a tendency to see Jesus (through the eyes of Kant) as the great 'enlightener' who came teach people how to build the Kingdom of God on Earth. By contrast, Schweitzer argued that Jesus was immersed in a Jewish apocalyptic thought-world. For a more recent treatment, see Bart Ehrman, *Jesus: Apocalyptic Prophet of the New Millennium* (OUP, 1999).

Robert P. Carroll's *When Prophecy Failed* (SCM Press, 1979) offers one account of the demise of the Old Testament prophetic tradition and the rise of the apocalyptic consciousness. Carroll uses the psychological theory of 'cognitive dissonance' to explain the tension between what the prophets were promising and real conditions of social hardship.

W. H. Vanstone's *The Stature of Waiting* (Darton, Longman and Todd, 1982) reflects on the faculty of waiting in relation to the passion narrative. Another relevant book is Alan Ecclestone's study of the French Catholic Charles Péguy, *Staircase for Silence*. Peguy was greatly influenced by Bergson and developed a distinctive theology of time and place.

There are a number of readily available texts by Simone Weil. Siân Miles (ed.), *Simone Weil: An Anthology* (Virago, 1986) has a good selection of material and a useful introduction. The two books from which I drew most were *Waiting for God* (HarperCollins Perennial Classics, 2001) and *Gravity and Grace* which has been republished in the Routledge Classics series (2002) along with *Oppression and Liberty* (2001) and *The Need for Roots* (2001). I also found E. W. F. Tomlin's short study, *Simone Weil* (Bowes and Bowes, 1954) a very insightful guide, although it is not easy to get hold of.

The classic volume of Benjamin's essays is *Illuminations* edited and introduced by Hannah Arendt (Pimlico, 1999). For anyone wanting to read further I would recommend Gary Smith (ed.), *Benjamin: Philosophy, Ethics, History* (University of Chicago Press 1989), which contains some excellent essays about Benjamin. I found Rolf Tiedemann's essay on Benjamin and historical materialism particularly useful.

Don Cupitt has written a great deal and his views have developed in a number of ways over the past 20 years. But three books that show clearly his apocalyptic temperament are *The Time Being* (SCM Press, 1992); *The Revelation of Being* (SCM Press, 1998); and *The Religion of Being* (SCM Press, 1998). I still find his *Taking Leave of God* (SCM Press, 2001) an exhilarating book, and it is essential reading for anyone trying to understand Cupitt's thought.

Ulrich Beck advances his theory of risk in *Risk Society: Towards a New Modernity* (Sage, 1992). Anthony Giddens' theory of an apocalyptic risk culture can be found in *Modernity and Self Identity: Self and Society in the Late Modern Age* (Polity Press, 1991). Barbara Adam's *Timescapes of Modernity* (Routledge, 1998) looks at time in relation to environmental threats.

Kairic Time

Phillip Sipora and James Baumlin have edited an excellent collection of essays on Kairic time: *Rhetoric and Kairos: Essays in History, Theory and Praxis* (State University of New York Press, 2002). This book also contains a comprehensive bibliography on the topic of *kairos*.

Nietzsche's discussion of time is not contained in one book. Burns and Rayment-Pickard (eds), *Philosophies of History* (Blackwell, 2000) has excerpts on time from Nietzsche's writing and an essay on Schopenhauer, Nietzsche and Kierkegaard on the subject of history. Ned Lukacher, *Time-Fetishes: The Secret History of Eternal Recurrence* (Duke University Press, 1998) is a quirky but entertaining book looking at kairic themes from ancient times to the present day. It includes an excellent chapter on Shakespeare and time.

Jean-Pierre de Caussade's *Self Abandonment to Divine Providence* (Fontana, 1971) left me rather nonplussed, but it is a spiritual 'classic' and arguably worth reading for that reason. T. S. Eliot's *Four Quartets* (Faber and Faber, 1995) offers an unmatched mystical view of time, place and journey. R. S. Thomas comes back again and again to themes of time, history, decay, pessimism, absence and the value of the moment. His poetry is infused with philosophy and we can see the strong influence of Bergson, and of Kierkegaard for whom the concept of 'the present' (*øiblikket*) is so important. Here are some of Thomas' poems that tackle the theme of time: 'The Presence'; 'The Message'; 'The Fly'; 'The Bank'; 'Song at the Year's Turning'; 'Welsh Landscape'; 'Look Out' and 'Balance'.

The literature on Proust is vast. I learned a great deal from Malcolm Bowie's *Proust Among the Stars* (Fontana, 1998), which has a chapter on time. I also enjoyed Edmund White's brilliant essay *Proust* (Phoenix, 1999). White judges Proust to be 'the first contemporary writer of the twentieth century, for he was the first to describe the permanent instability of our times'. If you can get hold of it, Ortega y Gasset's essay 'Time, Distance and Form in the Art of Proust' *(Hudson Review,* vol. XI, no. 4, 1958–9), written just after Proust's death in 1922, describes Proust's 'microscopic' vision of time.

If you like Ortega y Gasset try his *History as a System* (Norton, 1941), which argues that 'life is a task' and that we must try to connect with 'the radical reality' of our own existence. Ortega's views were typical of the existentialist interest in time. Heidegger's *Being and Time* (Blackwell, 1978) is perhaps the most important book in this respect. Søren Kierkegaard, Karl Jaspers and Jean-Paul Sartre all felt that the secret of human time could only be accessed through present existence.

Prophetic Time

Selections from Kant's essays on universal history can be found in Burns and Rayment-Pickard (eds), *Philosophies of History* (Blackwell, 2000) along with commentary on the so-called 'Enlightenment view of history'. Karl Popper uses the term 'prophetic' history in a more tightly-defined way than I do here, but Chapter 25 ('Has History any Meaning') of *The Open Society and its Enemies* (Routledge, 2002) is worth reading.

A good place to start with Hegel is the Introduction to his *Philosophy of History.* I found Joseph McCarney's *Hegel on History* (Routledge, 2000) a clear and concise guide to the subject. Volume 1 of Leszek Kolakowski's *Main Currents of Marxism* (OUP, 1978) has first rate sections on Hegel's theory of history (1:13–14). Kolakowski connects Hegel and Marx with a biblical tradition of dialectical thought. In fact Marx's theory of history provides a good avenue into Hegel's thinking.

Habermas is not an easy read, but the ideas are important. Volume 3 of

Kolakowski's *Main Currents of Marxism* has a few pages on Habermas' early thought. There is a summary of his theory of history and excerpts from his writing in Burns and Rayment-Pickard (eds), *Philosophies of History* (Blackwell, 2000). Jürgen Habermas, *Postmetaphysical Thinking* (MIT Press, 1992) contains some easier pieces and William Outhwaite's *The Habermas Reader* (Polity Press, 1996) has good selections on Habermas' theory of communication and on his re-working of Marx's 'historical materialism'.

David Tracy's *Plurality and Ambiguity* (SCM Press, 1987) is a wonderful book that I keep coming back to. Tracy argues that the future of Christianity hinges upon the development of an ethic of conversation – a conclusion which seems to me to be increasingly irresistible.

Fiction

There is a wealth of fictional works dealing with time, and I read a few while researching this book. I discuss Proust, Shakespeare and Pynchon at length in the book. I also refer to Graham Swift's *Waterland*, but could also have mentioned his *Last Orders* (Picador, 1997). In *The Magic Mountain* Thomas Mann reflects upon death, decay and the passage of time. The novel is set in a sanatorium, where the hero Hans Castorp is forced to re-think his attitudes to life, death and time. Mann described the book as 'a time-romance' and the novel contains a number of philosophical meditations on time: on the nature of subjective time; whether time can be narrated; whether time is a kind of disease; on the links between past, present and future. Mann was a pessimist inspired by his love of Schopenhauer's philosophy. Bleaker still than Thomas Mann is Thomas Hardy for whom tragedy is the very stuff of life. I mention *Jude the Obscure* (Penguin, 1994), but the tragic theme runs through all of his writing. Virginia Woolf's *Mrs Dalloway* (Penguin, 1996) explores the spaces between public and private time – a theme which is explored further in *The Hours* (2002, dir: Stephen Daldry) a complex film that draws both upon the novel by Michael Cunningham and Woolf's own life. Martin Amis' *Time's Arrow* is a breathtaking experiment in reversing time to effect an ironic and disturbing re-evaluation of human tragedy: viewed *backwards* death is birth, and so on. Amis acknowledges his debt to Kurt Vonnegut who reverses the bombing of Dresden in *Slaughterhouse 5*. Vonnegut plays with the question of time in two other novels: *Timequake* and *Cat's Cradle*. People either love Vonnegut or hate him and I fall into the former category. Philip K. Dick's *Counter-Clock World* (Voyager, 2002) imagines that history suddenly reverses, bringing the dead to life, turning eating into excretion and vice-versa. *Counter-Clock World* is full of theological resonances, with title quotations from Duns Scotus and St Augustine. Paul Fiddes analyses a range of fictional treatments of eschatology in *The Promised End* (Blackwell, 2000).

Science

There are many good popular books about the science of time. The best known is Stephen Hawking's *A Brief History of Time* (Bantam, 1988), but more accessible and wide-ranging is Paul Davies, *About Time* (Penguin, 1995). There is an excellent chapter on the arrow of time in Roger Penrose's *The Emperor's New Mind* (OUP, 1989). Julian Barbour's *The End of Time* (Phoenix, 1999) offers a scientific argument that time does not exist.

General

Katinka Ridderbos (ed.), *Time* (CUP, 2002) contains a broad range of scientific, philosophical and cultural essays. David S. Landes, *Revolution in Time* (Viking, 1983) is a long but fascinating history of clocks. E. G. Richards, *Mapping Time* (OUP, 1998) gives a cultural and historical survey of the calendar. Kristen Lippencott (ed.), *The Story of Time* (Merrell Holberton, 2000) contains a fascinating range of essays on a wide range of topics.

There are a number of useful anthologies of the philosophy of time and history, containing useful bibliographies. Charles M. Sherover (ed.), *The Human Experience of Time* (Northwestern, 2001) has selections from most of the key texts and thinkers; Robin Le Poidevin and Murray MacBeath (eds), *The Philosophy of Time* (OUP, 1993) offers a selection of texts from the analytical tradition. Donald Kelley (ed.), *Versions of History from Antiquity to Enlightenment,* (Yale University Press, 1991) combined with Robert Burns and Hugh Rayment-Pickard (eds), *Philosophies of History: from Enlightenment to Postmodernity,* (Blackwell, 2000) will give you a rich survey of texts from the whole gamut of Western philosophy of history. Philip Turetsky's *Time* (Routledge, 1998) is not an anthology, but offers a good (if not very readable) survey of philosophical thought about time. Gordon Graham, *The Shape of the Past* (OUP, 1997) is a more accessible book that offers a number of models or shapes that history can take.

Other Quoted Material

Adams, Douglas, *The Hitchhiker's Guide to the Galaxy* (Tor Books, 1988)

Adorno, Theodor, 'Progress' in Gary Smith (ed.), *Benjamin: Philosophy, Ethics, History* (University of Chicago Press, 1989)

Altizer, Thomas, *Genesis and Apocalypse* (Westminster/John Knox Press, 1990)

Amis, Martin, 'The Time Disease' in *Einstein's Monsters* (Penguin, 1988)

Amis, Martin, *Time's Arrow* (Vintage, 2003)

Aristotle, *Nicomachean Ethics* (OUP, 2002)

Atwood, Margaret, *The Handmaid's Tale* (Vintage, 1996)

Auden, W. H., *For the Time Being* (Faber and Faber, 1945)

Auden, W. H., 'Time is our choice of How to love and Why' in *For the Time Being.*

Ballard, J. G., *Crash* (Vintage, 1995)

Baudelaire, Charles, *Intimate Journals* (Penguin Books, 1995)

Baudrillard, Jean, 'Objects, Images and the Possibilities of Aesthetic Illusion' in *Art and Artefact* (Sage, 1997)

Beckett, Samuel, *The Shorter Plays: With Revised Texts for Footfalls, Come and Go, and What Where* (Faber and Faber, 1999)

Benjamin, Walter, 'Theses on the Philosophy of History' in *Illuminations* (Pimlico, 1999)

Benjamin, Walter, *Arcades Project* (Harvard University Press, 2002)

Bergson, Henri, *The Creative Mind* (Citadel Press, 2002)

Blake, William, 'The Rose' and 'With Happiness stretch'd across the hills' in *Collected Poems* (Routledge Classics, 2002)

Borges, Jorge Louis, 'The Garden of Forked Paths' in *Collected Fictions* (Penguin Modern Classics, 1999)

Brecht, Bertolt, 'In the Dark Times' in *Poems 1913–1956* (Methuen, 2000)

Burns, Robert, 'Open the Door to me, Oh' in *Complete Poems and Songs of Robert Burns* (Geddes & Grosset, 2002)

Cartier-Bresson, Henri, *The Decisive Moment* (Simon and Schuster, 1952)

Chesterton, G. K., in *The Collected Works of G K Chesterton* (Ignatius Press, 2001)

Cicero cited in Phillip Sipora and James Baumlin (eds), *Rhetoric and Kairos: Essays in History, Theory and Praxis* (State University of New York Press, 2002)

Conrad, Joseph, *Nostromo* (Penguin Books, 1994)

Conrad, Joseph, *The Secret Agent* (Penguin, 2000)

Cullmann, Oscar, *Christ and Time* (Gordon Press Publishers, 1977)

Cupitt, Don, *The Time Being* (SCM Press, 1992)

Derrida, Jacques, *Given Time* (University of Chicago Press, 1994)

Derrida, Jacques, *Politics of Friendship* (Verso Books, 1997)

Duffy, Carol Ann, *Mean Time* (Anvil Press Poetry, 1998)

Ecclestone, Alan, *A Staircase to Silence* (Darton, Longman & Todd, 1977)

Eco, Umberto, 'Times' in Kristen Lippencott (ed.), *The Story of Time* (Merrell Holberton, 2000)

Emerson, Ralph Waldo, *Essays* (Phoenix, 1995)

Faulkner, William, *Requiem for a Nun* (Chatto and Windus, 1975)

Feuerbach, Ludwig, *The Essence of Christianity* (Prometheus Books UK, 1989)

Fox, Matthew, *Original Blessing* (Bear & Company, 1996)

Fromm, Erich, *To Have or To Be* (Abacus, 1987)

Frye, Northrop, *The Double Vision* (University of Toronto Press, 1991)

Gay, Peter, *The Enlightenment: An Interpretation* (W. W. Norton, 1995)

Genet, Jean, *Miracle of the Rose* (Penguin, 1971)

Hegel, G. W. F., *The Philosophy of History* (Peter Smith Publishing, 1976)

Hegel, G. W. F., *The Philosophy of Nature* (OUP, 1970)

Heidegger, Martin, 'On the Experience of Thinking' in *Poetry, Language, Thought* (HarperCollins, 1975)

Heidegger, Martin, *Introduction to Metaphysics* (Yale University Press, 1987)

Herder, J. F., *Yet Another Philosophy of History* (1774) in *Against Pure Reason: Writings on Religion, Language and History* (Fortress Press, 1993). Also excerpted in Burns and Rayment-Pickard (eds), *Philosophies of History* (Blackwell, 2000)

Hopkins, Gerard Manley, 'Pied Beauty' in *Major Poems* (Everyman Edition, Dent, 1979)

Horkheimer, Max and Adorno, Theodor, *The Dialectic of Enlightenment* (Stanford University Press, 2002)

Hughes, Ted, *Crow* (Faber and Faber, 1999)

Hugo, Victor, *L'Autographe* (cited by Walter Benjamin in his *Arcades Project*, Harvard University Press, 2002)

Huxley, Aldous, *Brave New World* (Flamingo, 1994)

Jaspers, Karl, *Tragedy is not Enough* (Shoe String Press, 1969)

Kant, Immanuel, *Berlin Monthly* see Burns and Rayment-Pickard (eds), *Philosophies of History* (Blackwell, 2000)

Kierkegaard, Søren, *Journals* (Harper & Row, 1959)

Lang, Fritz, *Metropolis* (Faber and Faber, 1990)

Lawrence, D. H., 'The Optimist' in *The Complete Poems of D. H. Lawrence* (Wordsworth Editions, 1994)

Lotze, H., 'Of Time' in *Metaphysics*, 1887. (Can be found in chapter 13 of M. Sherover (ed.), *The Human Experience of Time* (Northwestern University Press, 2001)

Mann, Thomas, *The Magic Mountain* (Vintage, 1996)

Marcus Aurelius, *Meditations* (Orion, 2003)

McTaggart, J. M. E., *The Nature of Existence* (Native American Book Distributors, 1968)

Marx, Karl, 'Theses on Feuerbach' in D. McLellan (ed.), *Karl Marx: Selected Writings* (OUP, 2000)

Maxwell, Glyn, *Time's Fool* (Picador, 2001)

Merleau-Ponty, Maurice, *Phenomenology of Perception* (Routledge, 1992)

Merton, Thomas, *Contemplative Prayer* (Darton, Longman & Todd, 1983)

Milton, John, 'On His Blindness' in *The Complete Poems* (Penguin, 1999)

Nash, Thomas, 'Song in Time of Pestilence' in *Works* (Blackwell, 1958)

Nietzsche, Friedrich, *The Gay Science* (Random House, 1974)

Nietzsche, Friedrich, *The Will to Power* (Random House USA, 1968)

Nietzsche, Friedrich, *Thus Spoke Zarathustra* (Prometheus Books UK, 1993)

Orwell, George, *Nineteen Eighty-Four* (Penguin, 1998)

Ovid, *Metamorphoses* (Oxford World Classics, 1998)

Piaget, Jean, *Principles of Genetic Epistemology* (Routledge, 1977)

Pickstock, Catherine, *After Writing* (Blackwell, 1997)

Poe, Edgar Allan, 'The Raven' in *The Complete Tales and Poems of Edgar Allan Poe* (Penguin Classics, 1982)

Proust, Marcel, *In Search of Lost Time* (Penguin, 2003)

Pullman, Philip, *His Dark Materials* (Scholastic, 2001)

Pynchon, Thomas, *Gravity's Rainbow* (Vintage, 1995)

Ranke, Leopold von *Histories of the Latin and Germanic Nations from 1494–1514*, reproduced in Fritz Stern, *The Varieties of History. From Voltaire to the Present* (Random House, 1972)

Reichenbach, Hans, *The Direction of Time* (University of California Press, 1991)

Sontag, Susan, *On Photography* (Penguin Books, 2002)

Spencer, Herbert, *Social Statics* (Robert Schalkenbach Foundation, 1995)

Swift, Graham, *Waterland* (Picador, 1992)

Thomas, R. S., 'Where?' in *Collected Poems* (Weidenfeld & Nicolson, 1995)

Tillich, Paul, *The Eternal Now* (SCM Press, 2003)

Tolle, Eckhart, *The Power of Now* (Hodder & Stoughton, 2001)

Tolstoy, L., remark to N. Gusev. For details and further discussion of Tolstoy's view of history see Isaiah Berlin's essay 'The Hedgehog and the Fox' which is collected with other essays in *The Proper Study of Mankind* (Chatto & Windus, 1977)

Vattimo, Gianni, *The End of Modernity* (Polity Press, 1991)

Vaughan, Henry, 'Content' in *The Complete Poems* (Penguin Classics, 1995)

Vaughan, Henry, 'The Evening Watch' in *The Complete Poems* (Penguin Classics, 1995)

Vonnegut, Kurt, *Slaughterhouse 5* (Vintage, 2003)

Walker, Henry, 'Christian Work and Workers' in *East London: Sketches of Christian Work and Workers* (P. Marcan, 1984)

Williams, William Carlos, *Paterson IV* (Penguin Books, 1990)

Woolf, Virginia, *Moments of Being: Autobiographical Writings* (Pimlico, 2002)

Yeats, W. B., 'The Second Coming' in *Collected Poems* (Picador, 1990)

Zizioulas, John, *Being as Communion* (Darton, Longman & Todd, 1985)

INDEX

143

INDEX

INDEX

142